INTERMEDIATE

WHAT'S IN A WORD?

Reading and Vocabulary Building

Samuela Eckstut Karen Sorensen

Longman

What's in a Word?: Reading and Vocabulary Building

Longman, 10 Bank Street, White Plains, N.Y. 10606

Associated companies:
Longman Group Ltd., London
Longman Cheshire Pty., Melbourne
Longman Paul Pty., Auckland
Copp Clark Pitman, Toronto

Credits appear on page 181.

Distributed in the United Kingdom by Longman Group Ltd., Longman House, Burnt Mill, Harlow, Essex CM20 2JE, England and by associated companies, branches, and representatives throughout the world.

Executive editor: Joanne Dresner
Development editor: Karen Davy, Penny Laporte
Production editor: Lisa Hutchins
Text design: Book Builders Incorporated
Cover design: Suzanne Lobel
Text art: Beckwith-Clark, Inc. and Book Builders Incorporated
Production supervisor: Anne Armeny

Library of Congress Cataloging in Publication Data
Eckstut, Samuela.
What's in a word? : reading and vocabulary building / Samuela Eckstut, Karen Sorensen.
p. cm.
ISBN 0-8013-0624-8
1. English language—Textbooks for foreign speakers. 2. Readers—1950- 3. Vocabulary. I. Sorensen, Karen. II. Title.
PE1128.E345 1992 91-38254
428.6'4—dc20 CIP

5 6 7 8 9 10-CRS-97 96

TABLE OF CONTENTS

TO THE STUDENT

When you have learned a word, what is it exactly that you have learned? Surely you have learned the meaning of the word. You should also have learned how to say the word correctly. (It is not very helpful if nobody can understand you when you use this new word.) Hopefully, you also know how to use the word correctly. (If the preposition *in* always follows the word but you use the preposition *for*, have you really learned everything about the word you should have learned?) Finally, have you learned whether you can use this word in all situations? (Should you use this word or expression when applying for a job, or is it a word usually used between friends and family?)

In this book you will practice all of these aspects of vocabulary learning. The book will also teach you how to use the vocabulary you already know in order to learn more. In addition, it will show you different ways of understanding unknown words you meet in your reading, and it will help you to use a monolingual, English–English, dictionary effectively. When you have finished this book, you will not only know more words but you will have learned many new vocabulary-building strategies which you can use in and out of English class.

Each unit begins with a text for you to read. The text introduces new words in context for you to study. It also provides a topic for you to discuss with the other members of your class. When you read the text, you should not try to understand every detail but just the writer's general points.

In order to do many of the exercises in this book, you will need to use an English–English dictionary. A dictionary written especially for learners of English would be best. Whichever dictionary you choose, be sure that it gives the pronunciation of words and that it has a pronunciation guide which shows the meaning of its pronunciation symbols.

How do you remember new words? We suggest that you keep some sort of vocabulary record. There are many systems; you should choose the one that suits you best. Some people use separate notebooks. Others use small cards (7½ cm × 12½ cm; 3 in. × 5 in.). Small cards have the advantage of being easier to carry around. Therefore, it would be easy to take them out and study them while waiting for a bus, for example.

How should you organize your words? Many people organize them alphabetically, as a dictionary does. Others organize them according to parts of speech, for example, all the nouns together, all the verbs together, and so on. Still others organize them according to subject matter. For example, they have a section for words related to health and another for words related to travel. Finally, there are people who organize their record according to which words they learned in class that day or that week.

Whichever method of organization you choose, your vocabulary record should contain the information which will help you learn your words most effectively. In the very least, it should contain the pronunciation of the word, the part of speech, the meaning of the word,* an example of the word in use—either in an example from the dictionary or in the sentence where you first met the word—and information about the grammar of the word. In addition, it is a good idea to include the word's derived forms. For example, if the word is a verb, is there a noun and/or adjective related to it? Below is an example of what an effective vocabulary entry looks like.

> Know /now/verb past: knew past participle: known
> Grammar: instransitive verb; also, transitive verb/+(that)/
> NOT be + verb-ing
>
> Meaning: to have information (about) in the mind
>
> Example: I know he's there because I saw him.
>
> Derived forms:
> noun – knowledge/'naldɪ/ʒ
> adjective – knowledgeable/'naldɪ/ʒəbəl/

*It is not a good idea to write down every meaning of the word that a dictionary gives. One word in English can have many different meanings, and if you write them all down, you may not learn any of them very well. Therefore, it is best to learn only the meaning of the word as it is used in the context in which you have met it.

TO THE TEACHER

What's in a Word? is designed to help intermediate students increase their active and passive vocabulary through presentation of lexical items in context and through practice and review. It also aims to sensitize students to different aspects of vocabulary learning and to introduce them to certain study habits useful for more effective learning.

The book consists of twelve units plus four reviews. Each unit should take a minimum of three class hours to complete and is divided into three sections. The three sections of each unit are described below.

A removable answer key is provided for the teacher and for students using the book on their own. The cassette, which contains recordings of the unit readings and the texts for dictation from the review units, reinforces sight and sound association.

PRESENTATION

This section begins with a warm-up activity to introduce the theme of the unit and, when appropriate, to introduce vocabulary that students will meet in the reading. Each reading has ten lexical items from a particular semantic field; alternatively, these lexical items are commonly used in connection with the semantic field though not necessarily restricted to it. Usefulness, need, and level were the primary criteria used in selecting these words and phrases. Vocabulary of which students have a passive understanding, but do not use correctly, has also been included.

The ten words and phrases presented in the reading are the focus of follow-up activities that guide the students to an understanding of the lexes based on their context, structure, and/or association with related words. The final activity in the Presentation section provides students with a chance to use the words and phrases actively in a communicative context.

EXPANSION

This section introduces additional words and phrases related to the ten lexical items introduced and practiced in the presentation section. It also focuses on distinguishing shades of meaning, sorting out differences between commonly confused words, and building on students' knowledge of word parts. Like the final activity in the Presentation section, the activity at the end of the expansion section provides students with a communicative context in which to practice many of the words and phrases introduced so far in the unit.

WORD STUDY

The final section in each unit asks students to look more analytically at some of the words they have practiced in the unit. It focuses on such areas as the grammar of words, pronunciation, spelling, and collocation. It also helps students develop skills for more efficient dictionary use.

We hope that the activities in *What's in a Word?* will not only be effective in helping students truly "know" the words they learn but will also stimulate students to approach vocabulary learning in a new way.

UNIT 1 ANGER

Do you know these words?

to have an argument	furious	to slam —
to be in a bad mood	annoyed	to grab — to snatch.
to lose one's temper		to shatter
to yell		
to scream		

PRESENTATION

1 List five words that come to mind when you say the word *anger*. Compare lists with another student and explain why you wrote these words.

1. ________ 2. ________ 3. ________ 4. ________ 5. ________

2 Talk about a time you felt very angry. Then read the following story.

In the story that follows, Dom DeLuise, an American comedian, remembers a night from his childhood. He describes the night his father got angry. Think about this as you read: Have you ever had a similar experience in your family?

Listen as you read the story.

The Night of the Fabulous Flying Pasta e Fagiolis

One of my favorite meals as a child was pasta e fagioli.[1] It was dinnertime and I had my napkin tucked under my chin, and my spoon was ready, clutched in my hot little hand. My mother had just put a huge potful of pasta e fagioli in a large serving bowl. My father was all cleaned up after work. I was enjoying the feel of the fresh clean tablecloth under my hands when Mamma got *annoyed* with something Papa did and they started to *have an argument.* I knew my father *was in a bad mood* and was tired and hungry, and I also knew that once we sat down and had some pasta e fagioli, everything was going to be all right. But the pasta never got to the table. My mother must have raised her voice and *yelled* at Papa because he got *furious.* He *lost his temper* and before we knew it, he had *grabbed* that giant serving bowl filled with my favorite pasta e fagioli and thrown it up and over his shoulder so that all the beans and macaroni went flying. They seemed somehow suspended in air for one magical moment, just like a slow-motion shot in the movies. But before I knew it the pieces of broken bowl *shattered* on the floor, then the walls, ceiling, lamps, stove, windows—even the curtains—were covered with pasta e fagioli! My father opened the door to the apartment *screaming* in his poor English, "I no see no thing like this my whole life!" He *slammed* the door behind him.

I thought, I never saw anything like this in my whole life either, Pop.

I can see myself sitting there with my napkin still tucked under my chin, the spoon still in my hand, with nothing to eat. The whole family was shocked. After a while we cleaned up the kitchen as best we could.

Months later, when I was changing a light bulb in the kitchen, I found a bean and a macaroni stuck to the ceiling to remind me of that evening. "Wow!" I thought. "He got that bean way up here?" For years, especially during spring cleaning, we kept finding beans and macaroni. When Papa was angry, he was angry.

Nowadays beans and macaroni is still one of my favorite dishes, but I never eat it without thinking back on the night in Brooklyn when we were visited by the "Fabulous Flying Pasta e Fagiolis."

[1] pasta e fagioli: an Italian food made of beans and macaroni

3 The pictures below show what happened in the story, but they are not in the correct order. Put the pictures in the correct order. Write the numbers 1 through 5 under the pictures. Then describe what is happening in each picture.

2 a. shattered

b. clutched . 1

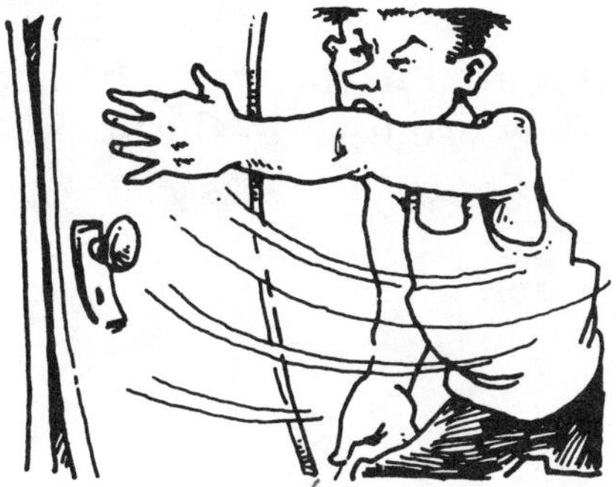

5 c. slammed

d. grabbed . 3

e. yelled

4 Ask another student these questions.

1. Whom do you know that often gets angry?
2. How do you know when this person is angry?
3. Do you remember one time when this person got very angry? What happened?

5 Are any of the words you listed in exercise 1 in the story? What do these words mean?

> **FOCUS ON GUESSING MEANING:** When you read, it is important to try to guess the meaning (or general meaning) of new words from the context.

6 The following words in *italics* appeared in the story on page 2. Try to guess their meaning from the way they are used in the story. Circle the correct answers.

1. Mamma was *annoyed*. How did she feel?
   - **a.** Sad
   - **b.** Sick
   - **c.** Angry
2. Mamma and Papa started to *have an argument*. What did they start to do?
   - **a.** Eat
   - **b.** Clean
   - **c.** Fight
3. Papa *was in a bad mood*. What didn't he feel like doing?
   - **a.** Talking to anyone anybody.
   - **b.** Having dinner
   - **c.** Getting washed
4. Mamma *yelled*. What did she do? yell out. Yell for Yell at
   - **a.** She spoke in a quiet voice.
   - **b.** She spoke in a loud voice.
   - **c.** She didn't speak at all.
5. Papa got *furious*. How did he feel? furios Mad. Rage.
   - **a.** Very tired
   - **b.** Very hungry
   - **c.** Very angry

6. Papa *lost his temper*. He was so angry that he could not
   a. control himself.
   b. eat.
   c. say a word.

7. Papa *grabbed* the bowl. What did he do with the bowl?
   a. He washed it.
   b. He took it from the table.
   c. He put more food in it.

8. The bowl *shattered*. What happened to the bowl?
   a. It broke.
   b. It got dirty.
   c. Nothing happened to it.

9. Papa was *screaming*. How was he speaking?
   a. In a quiet voice
   b. In a loud voice
   c. In a normal voice

10. Papa *slammed* the door. What did Papa do?
    a. He made a loud noise when he closed the door.
    b. He closed the door very quietly.
    c. He damaged the door when he closed it.

FOCUS ON SYNONYMS: Some words may be similar. However, this does not mean that they have the exact same meaning or that they can be used in the exact same way.

7 Look at the pairs of words and phrases in the boxes. How are they different in meaning from each other? Write the correct answer to each question in the blank.

Example: lost his temper   got angry

Which phrase shows that the person was very angry and started shouting? lost his temper

1. lost her temper   got annoyed

   Which phrase shows that the person became a little angry? ______

2. argument   fight

   Which word means that people use only words to show anger? ______

3. talk   yell

   Which word shows "in a loud voice"? ______

4. | angry furious |

Which word shows uncontrolled anger? furious

5. | grab take |

Which word shows sudden movement? grab (quigly.)

6. | shatter break |

Which word shows that there are many little pieces? Shatter,

7. | scream talk |

Which word shows "in a loud voice"? Scream

8. | shut slam |

Which word often shows that a person is angry? slam.

8 Look at the words in *italics* in the story on page 2. Some words talk about feelings of anger. Other words describe actions sometimes or always connected with anger. Put the italicized words from the story in the correct column.

Feelings of Anger	Words Sometimes Connected with Anger	Words Always Connected with Anger
1. Scream	3. furious	9. ______
2. fight	4. annoyed	10. ______
	5. ______	
	6. ______	
	7. ______	
	8. ______	

9 Play the Word Game. Get into groups of four or five. You will need to have a die (or six pieces of paper with the numbers 1 to 6 written on them). One student in each group throws the die twice (or chooses two pieces of paper). The first number is for words in box A; the second number is for words in box B. The student must think of a situation using the two words. Then it is the next student's turn. The first student who uses all the words in box A is the winner.

Example: 2 (furious); 5 (parking space)
Possible answer: One driver was *furious* with another driver for taking the *parking space* he had been waiting for.

A		B	
1. annoyed	4. grab	1. school	4. bed
2. furious	5. have an argument	2. bus	5. parking space
3. in a bad mood	6. slam	3. bank	6. street

EXPANSION

FOCUS ON EXPRESSIONS: You can learn several new expressions when you learn one new word.

10 **A.** The words and expressions in the diagram come from *temper.* Study them and then read the sentences below. Try to guess the meanings of these words and expressions. Circle the correct answers.

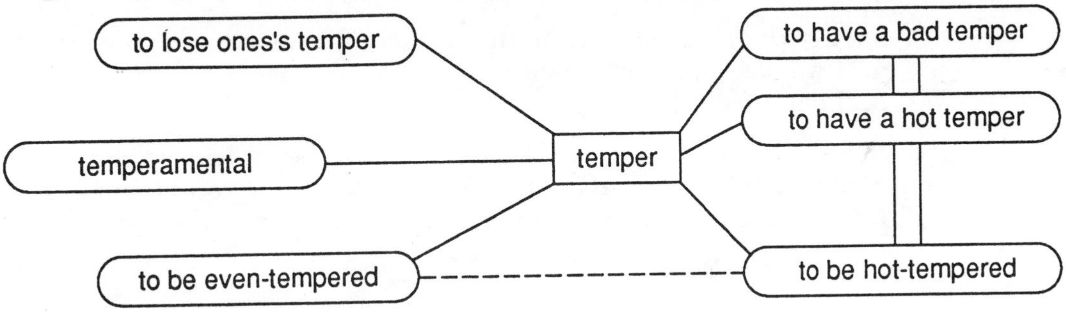

Example: I waited in line at the post office for twenty-five minutes. When I was then told that I was in the wrong line, I *lost my temper.*

a. I smiled and said, "Thank you."
b. I got angry and started shouting.

1. He tries not to do anything wrong at work because his boss *has a bad temper.*
a. His boss gets angry easily and shouts a lot.
b. His boss is very friendly and always wants to help.

2. People don't like to spend time with Sue because she *is hot-tempered.*
a. Sue gets angry easily and shouts a lot.
b. Sue is very friendly and always wants to help.

3. She is easy to get along with because she *is* so *even-tempered.*
a. She is a calm person and doesn't get angry easily.
b. She gets angry easily and shouts a lot.

4. The actor is so *temperamental* that nobody wants to work with him.
   a. The actor is always friendly and tells funny stories.
   b. One minute the actor is friendly; the next minute he is angry and complaining about something.

B. The words and expressions in the diagram come from *mood*. Study them and then read the sentences below. Try to guess the meanings of these words and expressions. Circle the correct answers.

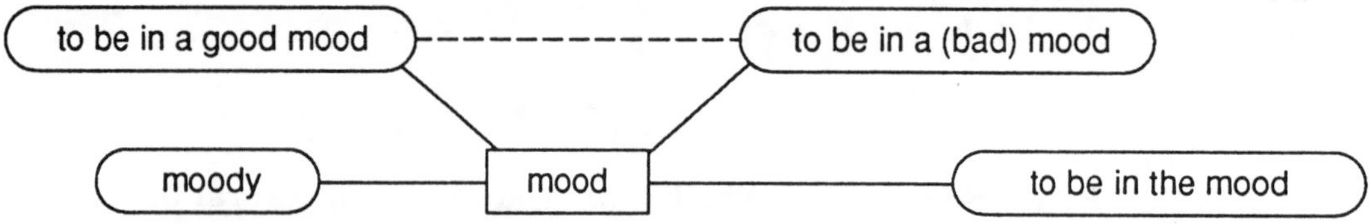

1. She'*s in a good mood* today. Look how she's smiling.
   a. She's angry.
   b. She's happy.
2. You'*re in a mood.* Did you have a bad day at work?
   a. You're not smiling; you don't want to talk; everything is annoying you.
   b. You're smiling; you want to talk a lot; you're happy to be with others.
3. I'*m not in the mood* to go to the movies. Why don't you go without me?
   a. I want to go to the movies.
   b. I don't feel like going to the movies.
4. She's nice, but she's so *moody* that she can be difficult to live with.
   a. She can be very happy and then suddenly she can become very sad.
   b. She is always friendly and happy to be around other people.

> **FOCUS ON TOPIC-RELATED WORDS:** It is helpful to learn words related to the same topic.

11 Look at the following expressions.

be fed up   put up with   blame   be someone's fault   can't stand

Find these expressions in the dialogue that follows and underline them. Check with another student or use your dictionary to be sure you understand the meaning and use of these expressions.

Mamma: I'm fed up . . . I'm fed up with you and the way you look at every woman who passes by.

Papa: You're fed up? All you do is complain, complain. I don't think I can put up with you and your complaining for another minute.

Mamma: I have every right to complain. If you spent more time working and less time looking at every pretty face that walks by, I wouldn't always have to worry if we have enough money for food.

Papa: Listen, don't blame me if we never have enough money. It's your fault. You spend it on all sorts of things we don't need. That dress . . . did you need that dress?

Mamma: So! You want every woman to be pretty but me!

Papa: Here we go again. I look at one woman and the world's going to end. I just can't stand it anymore.

12 Husbands and wives are not the only family members who have arguments. Brothers and sisters often do too. With another student, use the expressions which you underlined in exercise 11 to write a dialogue between a brother and a sister, two brothers, or two sisters. When you have finished, compare dialogues with other students.

13 **A.** Write *T* if the sentence is true about you. Write *F* if it is false. Then tell another student what you wrote and why.

1. I *lose my temper* easily. ______
2. I *am in a bad mood* when I wake up in the morning. ______
3. I walk out and *slam* the door if I'm angry with someone. ______
4. I often *have arguments* with the people I live with. ______
5. I get *annoyed* if someone comes an hour late for an appointment. ______
6. I rarely *yell* in public. ______
7. I am *furious* when someone telephones at 3 A.M. ______
8. I *can't stand* people who are unkind to animals. ______
9. It *is* always *my fault* if I do not do well on a test. ______
10. I'm a *moody* person. ______
11. I can't *put up with* cigarette smoke in my home. ______

B. Copy three true sentences and two false sentences about yourself from exercise 13A. (Or write your own sentences using the words in *italics* from 13A.) Then read your sentences to others in your class. They must guess which two sentences are false.

WORD STUDY

FOCUS ON THE GRAMMAR OF WORDS: Dictionaries have important grammar information to help you use new words correctly.

A dictionary will tell you

- if a verb [*v*] is transitive [T] or if it is intransitive [I].
  Transitive verbs are followed by a direct object. That is why the sentence *She* ***made*** is not correct. Intransitive verbs are not followed by an object. That is why the sentence *She just* ***sat it*** is not correct.
- if a noun [*n*] is countable [C] or if it is uncountable [U].
  Countable nouns can be singular (***An argument is*** *always unpleasant*) or plural (***Arguments are*** *always unpleasant*).
  Uncountable nouns are neither singular nor plural, but they are used with a singular verb (*His* ***anger was*** *uncontrollable*).
- if a verb is followed by a certain preposition (*about, for, in, on,* etc.).
  Some verbs can be followed by one or more prepositions (*I* ***looked at*** *the pasta and beans all over the kitchen*).

14 **A.** The following words appear in this unit. Study the grammar information which comes before each definition.

argument *n* [C] a disagreement, especially one that is noisy
blame *v* **blamed, blaming** [T *for, on*] to consider (someone) responsible for (something bad)
anger *n* [U] a fierce feeling of displeasure, usually leading to a desire to hurt or stop the person or thing causing it
scream *v* (I) to cry out loudly in a high note, in fear, pain, excitement, or sometimes laughter
yell *v* [I;T *at, out*] to say, shout, or cry loudly

B. The sentences in column A are correct. The sentences in column B are not correct. In each blank write the grammar information from the dictionary entry which shows why each sentence in column B is wrong.

Example: put *v* **put, putting** [T] to move to a stated place

A	B	
My mother put it in a bowl.	My mother put in a bowl.	[T]

[*Put* is transitive [T]. It must have an object. *Put* has no object in the sentence in column B.]

	A	B	
1.	I'm not talking to my brother; I had an argument with him.	I'm not talking to my brother; I had argument with him.	______
2.	I didn't do anything wrong; don't blame me.	I didn't do anything wrong; don't blame.	______
3.	She blamed me for something I didn't do.	She blamed me about something I didn't do.	______
4.	The bus driver blamed the accident on the truck driver.	The bus driver blamed the accident to the truck driver.	______
5.	I was sometimes afraid of my parents' anger.	I was sometimes afraid of my parents' angers.	______
6.	Papa screamed when he got angry.	Papa screamed it when he got angry.	______
7.	"I will yell at you if you touch this," Papa said.	"I will yell to you if you touch this," Papa said.	______

FOCUS ON SPELLING: There are certain rules that will help you spell correctly.

Verbs which have only one syllable and end in a single vowel and consonant (except *y*) usually double the final consonant before adding *-ed* or *-ing*.

sl<u>am</u> + ed = sla<u>mme</u>d (He slammed the door.)
sl<u>am</u> + ing = sla<u>mmi</u>ng (Why is she always slamming the door?)

Verbs of two syllables that end in a single vowel and consonant also usually double the final consonant before adding *-ed* or *-ing* when the stress is on the second syllable.

adMI<u>T</u> + ed = admi<u>t</u>ted (He admitted that he was wrong.)

15 Add *-ed* and *-ing* to these verbs. Be sure to spell them correctly. Use your dictionary if necessary.

Verb	***-ed***	***-ing***
admit	admitted	admitting
anger		
annoy		
grab		
scream		
shatter		
shout		
slam		
yell		

UNIT 2

RIGHT AND WRONG

Do you know these words?

moral	sympathetic	to do a favor	duty
grateful	be obligated	to relieve	conscience
irritated	concerned		

PRESENTATION

1 Choose six words from the list below which you think of as *good words* and six words which you think of as *bad words*. Write these words in the appropriate column. Then explain your choices to another student.

businesspeople tell a lie government homeless honest
injure law suffer religion enemy work hard force

Good Words	Bad Words
1. law	1. injure
2. Religion	2. Tell a lie
3. honest	3. homeless.
4. law.	4. enemy.
5. businesspeople	5. suffer.
6. Government	6. force.

2 This unit's reading is a questionnaire entitled "What Are Your Values?" The word *value* has several meanings. In each of the following sentences, *value* is used differently.

a. Property *values* have gone down from $150,000 to $100,000.
b. This map was of great *value* when we were lost.
c. Sometimes I wonder if you have any *values*. Do you know the difference between right and wrong?

Read the questionnaire. Then circle the letter of the sentence above in which the meaning of *value* is the same as in the title of the questionnaire.

Listen as you read the questionnaire. Do not answer the questions yet.

What Are Your Values?

People have different values. How much do you agree with each of the following statements? There are five possible answers: Strongly Agree (1), Agree (2), Neutral (3), Disagree (4), Strongly Disagree (5).

1. I feel a *moral duty* to help people who suffer.

Strongly Agree **Strongly Disagree**
1 2 3 4 5

2. If they obey the law, businesspeople should do as they like.

1 2 3 4 5

3. I would *do a favor* for a person who needs it, even if she/he has not been *grateful* for past *favors*.

1 2 3 4 5

4. I often become more *irritated* than *sympathetic* when I see someone crying.

1 2 3 4 5

5. Individuals can do little to *relieve* suffering in the world.

1 2 3 4 5

6. My *conscience* bothers me when I see homeless people on the street.

1 2 3 4 5

7. People from different religions and countries are different in basic ways.

1 2 3 4 5

8. Generally speaking, people won't work hard unless they are forced to.

1 2 3 4 5

9. Most people are basically good.

1 2 3 4 5

10. People should never make excuses for lying.

Strongly Agree			**Strongly Disagree**	
1	**2**	**3**	**4**	**5**

11. If a friend of mine wanted to injure an enemy of his/hers, I would *be obligated* to stop him/her.

1 **2** **3** **4** **5**

12. I am *concerned* about human beings everywhere in the world.

1 **2** **3** **4** **5**

13. Most people who get ahead in this world are honest, good people.

1 **2** **3** **4** **5**

14. Most people with serious problems caused their own problems.

1 **2** **3** **4** **5**

15. All people have the same basic needs and desires.

1 **2** **3** **4** **5**

FOCUS ON GUESSING MEANING: When you try to guess the meaning (or general meaning) of a new word, it is important to know what part of speech the word is. Is it a noun, adjective, verb, or adverb?

3 Find the following words in the questionnaire. If the word is used in the text as a noun, write *n* next to it. If it is used as an adjective, write *adj*. If it is used as a verb, write *v*.

1. concerned adj.

2. conscience __________

3. duty __________

4. do a favor adj.

5. grateful __________

6. irritated adj.

7. moral __________

8. be obligated adj.

9. relieve v.

10. sympathetic __________

4 **A.** Match the words in column A with their meanings in column B.

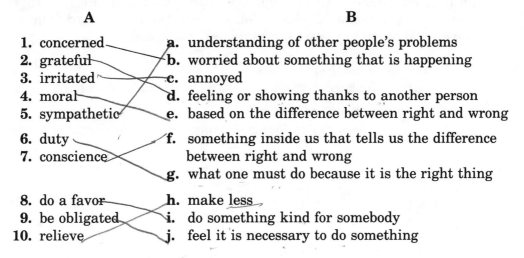

A	B
1. concerned	a. understanding of other people's problems
2. grateful	b. worried about something that is happening
3. irritated	c. annoyed
4. moral	d. feeling or showing thanks to another person
5. sympathetic	e. based on the difference between right and wrong
6. duty	f. something inside us that tells us the difference between right and wrong
7. conscience	g. what one must do because it is the right thing
8. do a favor	h. make less
9. be obligated	i. do something kind for somebody
10. relieve	j. feel it is necessary to do something

B. Refer back to the meaning of the words in exercise 4A and answer the following questions. When you have finished, ask your partner the questions.

1. Are you concerned about the drug problem in many parts of the world?
2. What are you grateful for?
3. When you are waiting in a line, do you get irritated by someone who tries to get in front of you?
4. Can you remember a time in your life when the moral thing to do was not the easy thing to do?
5. Are you sympathetic to the problems of poor people?
6. Do you think it is your duty to take care of your parents when they get old?
7. Does your conscience bother you if you tell a lie?
8. What was the last time you did a favor for someone?
9. Are your parents obligated to take care of you for your whole life?
10. What can governments do to relieve the suffering of hungry people in the world?

5 Read the questionnaire on pages 15 and 16 again and answer the questions. Circle the numbers that best describe your opinion or how you see yourself. Then compare answers with other students.

6 Which of the words in column B do you associate with the people in column A? Choose an appropriate word from column B and write the reason for your choice. (Note: You can use the same word from column B more than once, but you should use all the words.)

Example: **a mother:** *concerned*
Reason: *A mother is often concerned about her children.*

a mother: *irritated*
Reason: *A mother gets irritated if her children don't listen to her.*

A	B
1. a child	**a.** concerned
2. a father	**b.** grateful
3. a friend	**c.** irritated
4. a mother	**d.** moral
5. an old person	**e.** sympathetic
6. a politician	**f.** duty
7. a religious person	**g.** conscience
8. a soldier	**h.** do a favor
9. a teacher	**i.** be obligated
	j. relieve suffering

1. ______________________________
2. ______________________________
3. ______________________________
4. ______________________________
5. ______________________________
6. ______________________________
7. ______________________________
8. ______________________________
9. ______________________________

EXPANSION

FOCUS ON DERIVED FORMS: When you learn a new word, it is useful to learn the other forms related to that word: the derived words.

7 **A.** Write the derived forms of the words in *italics*. (Use a dictionary if you need help and be sure to check the pronunciation of the derived words.)

Adjective	Noun	Verb	Adverb
1. dutiful	*duty*		
grateful	2. ________		3. ________
irritated	4. ________	5. ________	
moral	6. ________		7. ________
	8. ________	*to be obligated*	
9. ________	10. ________	*to relieve*	
sympathetic	11. ________	12. ________	

B. Complete the paragraph with words from exercise 7A.

In many countries, old people no matter how ill or poor are taken care of by their families. My friend from China cannot understand why some Americans get upset and think of taking care of their parents as an ________ (1). She wonders how people do not feel ________ (2) for those who cannot look after themselves. She can't understand Americans who feel a sense of ________ (3) and ________ (4) when a nursing home agrees to take their parents. She believes that leaving the elderly to live the rest of their lives among strangers is ________ (5) wrong. For her, taking care of the elderly is not just a matter of ________ (6); it is a matter of conscience.

> **FOCUS ON EXPRESSIONS:** You can learn new expressions when you learn one new word.

8 Look at the common expressions with *conscience* on page 20. Study them and then read the following sentences. Try to guess the meanings of these expressions. Circle the correct answers.

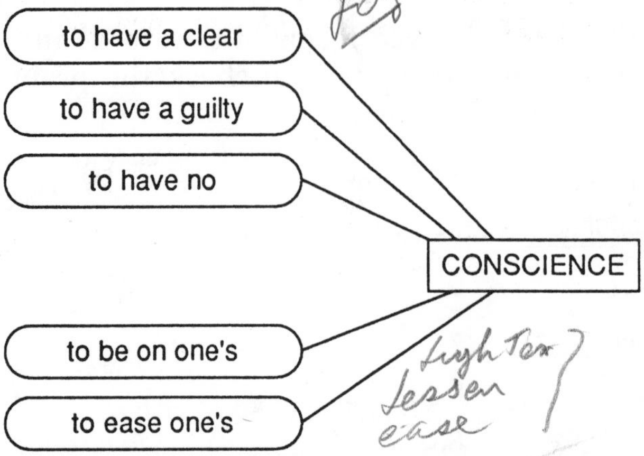

Example: I *have a clear conscience* about what happened. Someone had to stop my brother from stealing again. Even if he is my brother, I had to report him to the police.

a. I'm not upset because I don't feel I did anything wrong.
b. I'm upset because I feel I did something wrong.

1. He has been acting strangely ever since he left his wife. He must *have a guilty conscience.*
   a. He's not upset because he doesn't feel he did anything wrong.
   b. He's upset because he feels he did something wrong.
2. She bought her husband a watch after she realized she'd forgotten his birthday. She must have been trying to *ease her conscience.*
   a. She did something wrong. She must have wanted to help herself feel less upset.
   b. She did something wrong. She must have wanted to make her husband feel upset.
3. Mickey *has no conscience.* He would steal from his own mother if she had anything valuable.
   a. Mickey does not do anything wrong.
   b. Mickey is unable to tell the difference between right and wrong.
4. Larry hasn't been able to sleep lately. That lie he told must still *be on his conscience.*
   a. He must be feeling bad because he is sick.
   b. He must be feeling bad because he did something wrong.

9 In groups of four to six students, use the words you have learned in this unit and follow the same format as the questionnaire on page 15 and 16 to write fifteen more questions about people's values. When your group has finished, exchange questions with another group and discuss your answers to the other group's questions.

WORD STUDY

> **FOCUS ON PHONETIC SYMBOLS:** You can use the dictionary to find out how to say a word in English, but different dictionaries use different symbols for phonetic spellings. It is important to become familiar with the symbols in your dictionary.

10 **A.** Study these boxes. Box A has the phonetic spellings for words from this unit. Box B shows how some of the symbols in these phonetic spellings are pronounced.

	A
concerned	/kən'sɜrnd/
grateful	/'gre^{y}tfəl/
favor	/'fe^{y}vər/
moral	/'mɔrəl, 'mɑrəl/
conscience	/'kɑnʃəns, 'kɑntʃəns/
relieve	/rɪ'li^{y}v/

B	
/ə/	**banana**
/ɜr/	**burn**
/e^{y}/	**say**
/ɑ/	**car**
/ɔ/	**horse**
/ɪ/	**bit**
/i^{y}/	**beat**

B. Now complete these sentences with information from box B above.

1. The *o* in *concerned* sounds the same as the first and third __a__ in __banana__.
2. The *er* in *concerned* sounds the same as __ur__ in __burn__.
3. The *a* in *grateful* and *favor* sounds the same as __a__ in __say__.
4. The *o* in *moral* can sound the same as __ɔoa__ in __car__. Or, it can sound the same as __ɔoa__ in __horse__.
5. The *a* in *moral* and the *ie* in *conscience* sound the same as the first and third __ɔoa__ in __banana__.
6. The *o* in *conscience* sounds the same as __a__ in __car__.
7. The first *e* in *relieve* sounds the same as __it__ in __bit__.
8. The *ie* in *relieve* sounds the same as __ee__ in __beat__.

C. Look up the words in box A from exercise 10A in your dictionary and copy the phonetic spelling of each word.

1. concerned /______/
2. grateful /______/
3. favor /______/
4. moral /______/
5. conscience /______/
6. relieve /______/

Are the phonetic symbols in your dictionary different from the symbols used in 10A? If they are different, which symbols are different?

> **FOCUS ON SYLLABLE STRESS:** To say a word correctly, it is important to know which syllable receives special force, or stress. A dictionary will tell you which syllable is stressed.

Notice that the dictionary uses /ˈ/ before the stressed syllable.

/kənˈsɜrnd/	This shows that the second syllable is stressed.
/ˈfeʸvər/	This shows that the first syllable is stressed.

11 Look at the phonetic spellings in box A in exercise 10A again. Which syllable is stressed in these words? Check (✔) the appropriate box.

	First Syllable Stressed	Second Syllable Stressed
1. concerned		✔
2. grateful	✔	
3. favor	✔	
4. moral	✔	
5. conscience	✔	
6. relieve		✔

Now practice saying the words with other students. They should tell you which syllable you have stressed: the first or the second.

FOCUS ON THE PRONUNCIATION OF DERIVED WORDS: The same letters in derived words are often pronounced differently.

12 **A.** Look up *gratitude, morality,* and *relief* in your dictionary and copy the phonetic spelling of each word.

1. gratitude /__________________/ 2. morality /__________________/

3. relief /__________________/

B. Compare the pronunciation of the derived words in 12A with the words in 10A. Then answer the following questions. Write Yes or No.

1. Does the *a* in *gratitude* have the same sound as the *a* in *grateful?* No
2. Is the same syllable stressed in *gratitude* and *grateful?* No
3. Does the *a* in *morality* have the same sound as the *a* in *moral?* No
4. Is the same syllable stressed in *morality* and *moral?* No
5. Does the *ie* in *relief* have the same sound as the *ie* in *relieve?* Yes
6. Is the same syllable stressed in *relief* and *relieve?* ______

Now practice saying the words.

FOCUS ON COLLOCATIONS: *Do* and *make* are similar in meaning, but they are used in different expressions. For example, we say *do a favor* but *make an excuse.*

13 **A.** Look at the words below. Write them under the correct verb.

(someone) a favor   an excuse   a decision   a mistake   a good job
a promise   money   friends   something wrong   one's duty

Do	Make
do (someone) a favor	make an excuse

B. Ask another student these questions.

1. When was the last time you asked someone to do you a favor?
2. What mistakes have you made recently?
3. How much money would you like to make?
4. Who usually makes the decisions in your family?
5. When was the last time you made a promise? What did you promise to do? Did you keep the promise or break it?
6. When was the last time you did something wrong? What did you do?
7. What excuse do you make if you don't do your homework?
8. What is the best way for someone in a new place to make friends?

UNIT 3

DRIVING

Do you know these words?

to run into	to maintain	to signal	a vehicle
to crash	to steer	to speed up	a sharp curve
to slow down			a fatal accident

PRESENTATION

1 How many parts of a car can you name? Look at the pictures and label these parts: brake, headlights, turn signal, gas pedal, steering wheel, windshield wipers. (Note: Do not label all the parts of the pictures yet.)

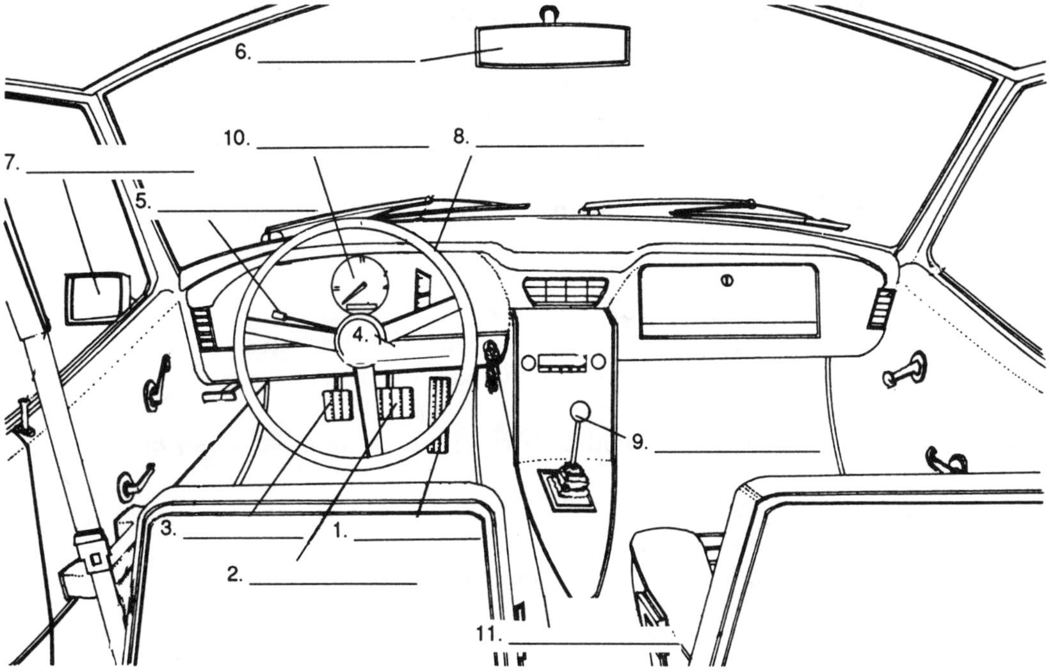

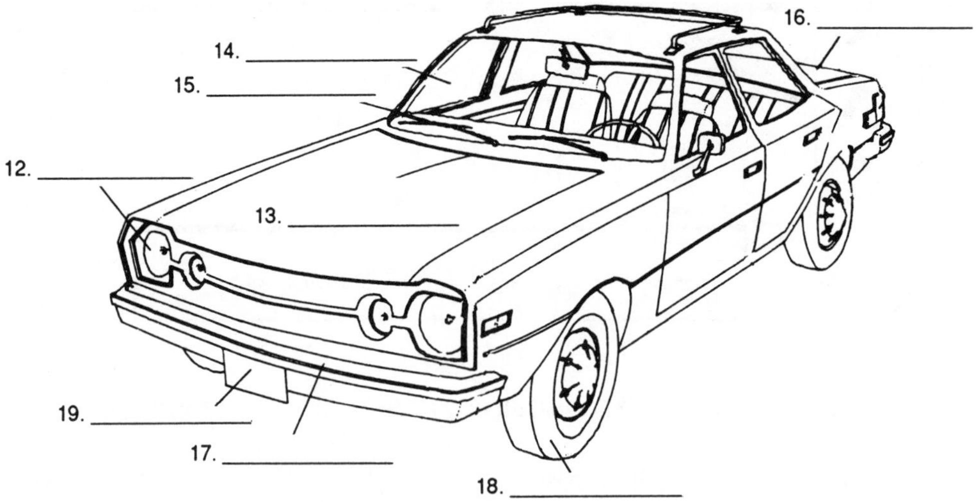

> **FOCUS ON GUESSING MEANING:** You can often guess the meaning (or general meaning) of a word if you look for clues which come before or after it.

2 A driving teacher is talking to a student. Read the conversation and try to guess the meaning of the words in *italics*. Circle the correct answer.

Student: When I pass the test, can I drive any kind of *vehicle*?
Teacher: No. Only a car. No motorcycles and no trucks.

1. A *vehicle* is something used on
   a. roads to carry people or things.
   b. water to carry people or things.

Teacher: Now, the first thing I want you to do is to keep both hands on the steering wheel and *steer* the car straight.

2. When you *steer* a car, you
   a. look straight ahead and watch the other cars.
   b. control the direction of the car.

Teacher: Now I want you to turn right. Remember to *signal*.

3. To *signal* means
   a. to turn right or left.
   b. to let someone know what you are going to do.

Teacher: Do you see that sign? It means you are near a *sharp curve*. Be careful and remember to *slow down*. There was a *fatal accident* here last week in which two people died.

4. What does a *sharp curve* look like?

a. 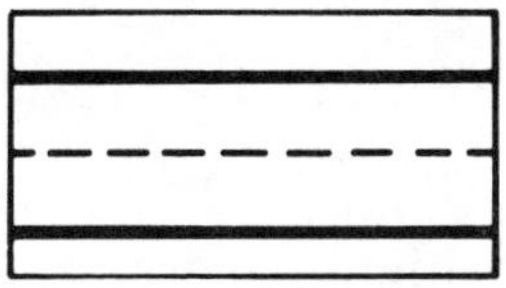

b. 

5. To *slow down* means
a. to go faster.
b. to go more slowly.

6. In a *fatal accident,* someone
a. dies.
b. hits another car.

Teacher: Now *maintain* your speed. Don't go any faster and don't slow down.

7. To *maintain* means
a. to change.
b. to continue to do as before.

Teacher: Okay, we're on the highway now. You must *speed up*. Don't go slowly on the highway. You can cause a *crash* if you go too slowly or too fast.

8. To *speed up* means
a. to go faster.
b. to go more slowly.

9. In a *crash,* a vehicle
a. goes slowly because it wants to turn.
b. hits, for example, another vehicle or a tree.

Teacher: Watch out! You're going to *run into* the bus . . . (BANG!)

10. When you *run into* something, you
a. hit it very hard.
b. run with it in your hand.

Listen as you read the driving quiz. Write *T* if you think the question is true. Write *F* if you think it is false.

Are You a Good Driver?

QUESTIONS

__T__ 1. Every time you turn on your windshield wipers, you should also turn on your headlights.

__F__ 2. When changing lanes, you should reduce your speed.

__T__ 3. If you think you are going to *run* head-on *into* another *vehicle*, it's better to drive off the road than to *crash*.

__F__ 4. When you come to a *sharp curve* in the road, you should *slow down* as you enter the *curve*.

ANSWERS

1. **True.** Turn on your lights and *slow down* whenever you use your wipers. You will see the road and traffic signs better, and other drivers will be able to see you better.
2. **False.** In normal situations and when not passing, *maintain* your speed as you *steer* gradually into a new lane. Be sure to *signal* well ahead of time.
3. **True.** Head-on *crashes* are the cause of most *fatal accidents*, so do everything you can to prevent one. Step on your brakes and, if possible, pull to the right, away from the car coming in the opposite direction. If necessary, drive off the road and try to hit something soft, like bushes. Even striking a tree or a parked car is better than hitting a moving vehicle.
4. **False.** *Slow down* <u>before</u> you enter the *curve*. Then *speed up* slightly as you finish the *curve*.

3 Check (✔) the correct column. Did the driving quiz test you on:

	Yes	No
1. why it is not good to drive fast?	______	______
2. what to do when it is raining?	______	______
3. what to do if the driver behind you is very close to your car?	______	______

	Yes	No
4. what to do if you want to go from the right lane to the middle lane?	______	______
5. what to do if you are about to hit another vehicle?	______	______
6. why you should not drink beer and then drive?	______	______
7. what to do when you drive, for example, on a mountain road?	______	______

4 Look at the following diagram. You were in car 3 and you saw an accident between a truck and a car. The police officer wants to ask you some questions. Work with another student and role-play the conversation. The police officer should ask all the questions below, but may add some more. Use the diagram to answer the police officer's questions. Use your imagination to add details.

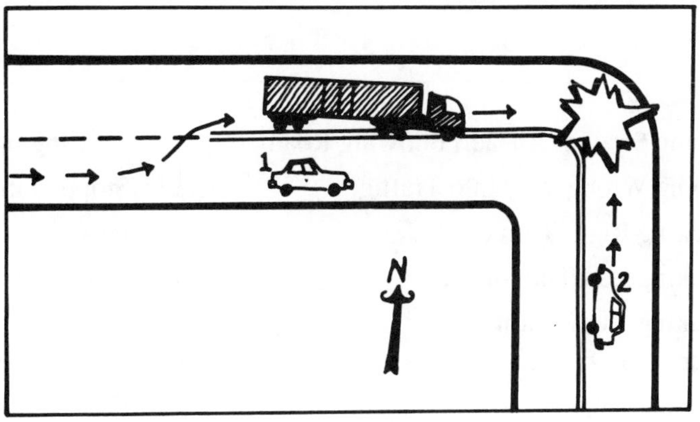

Officer: Can you tell me what happened?

You: 1. ______________________________

Officer: How fast were you going when the truck decided to pass you?

You: 2. ______________________________

Officer: How fast do you think the truck was going?

You: 3. ______________________________

Officer: Did you maintain your speed as the truck passed you? Or did you slow down?

You: 4. ______________________________

Officer: When you saw the car coming in the other lane, what did you do?

You: 5. ______________________________

Officer: Could you tell if either driver did anything to avoid the crash?

You: 6. ______________________________

Officer: Thank you. You will be sent an accident report form to complete.

5 Now look at the accident report form. The police officer filled in boxes A and B, which describe the actions of the two vehicles involved in the accident. In the lines below, describe how the accident happened.

ACCIDENT REPORT FORM

DIRECTIONS

Use Box A for the Vehicle That Caused the Accident.
Use Box B for the Other Vehicle.

A. 14, 15

B. 1, 13

1. Going Straight Ahead/Following Road
2. Going Wrong Way into Traffic
3. Making Right Turn on Red
4. Making Left Turn on Red
5. Making Right Turn
6. Making Left Turn
7. Making U-Turn
8. Starting from Parked Position
9. Starting in Traffic
10. Slowing in Traffic
11. Stopped in Traffic
12. Parked
13. Avoiding Vehicle, Object, Pedestrian in Road
14. Changing Lanes
15. Passing
16. Merging
17. Backing
18. OTHER ACTION

DESCRIBE ACCIDENT IN ENOUGH DETAIL TO SHOW CAUSES.

EXPANSION

> **FOCUS ON TWO-WORD VERBS:** In English there are many common verbs with two parts. The meaning of a two-word verb is often very different from the meanings of the two words taken separately. For example, to *run into* means to "hit something with a vehicle."

6 **A.** Read the following story. Try to guess the meanings of the underlined verbs.

Sometimes I wonder why I ever wanted to drive. This morning as I was backing up [1] the car, I hit the car behind me. After I dropped off [2] my children at their school, I started driving to a small town thirty miles away, where I had an appointment. I was driving along a beautiful, quiet country road. Suddenly, I saw some chickens crossing the road. Before I knew it, I had run over [3] one of them, and the farmer ran out of her house shaking her fist at me. It seemed country roads were not so peaceful after all, and I decided to take the highway instead. I turned off [4] at the third exit, and before I knew it there was a police car behind me. The policeman gave me a $150 ticket for going through [5] a stop sign. I swear I didn't see it. Besides, that's a dumb place to put a stop sign. Anyway, to make a bad day even worse, on my way home after I picked up [6] my children from school, my car broke down [7]. It cost me $65 to tow it to the nearest mechanic and another $400 to get it fixed. Next time I'm going to take a taxi.

B. Match the words in column A with their meanings in column B.

A	B
1. back up	a. stop working
2. drop off	b. hit and drive over
3. run over	c. go and get
4. turn off	d. leave
5. go through	e. move backwards
6. pick up	f. leave the road
7. break down	g. not stop at

7 Play Tic-Tac-Toe with a partner. One player is *X*, and the other player is *O*. *X* chooses a two-word verb and uses it in a sentence. If the sentence is correct, put an *X* on the verb. Then *O* takes a turn. The first player to have three *X*'s or three *O*'s in a straight line (—, |, \, or /) is the winner.

break down	run over	run into
turn off	back up	drop off
pick up	go through	turn on

FOCUS ON TOPIC-RELATED WORDS: It is helpful to learn words related to the same topic.

8 Look at the pictures on pages 25 and 26 again, and label the following parts of a car. Use your dictionary to check the pronunciation of these words.

bumper	horn	rearview mirror	tire
clutch	hood	sideview mirror	trunk
gear shift	license plate	speedometer	windshield
ignition			

FOCUS ON COMPOUND NOUNS: Nouns in English can be formed by combining a noun with another noun (*headlight*, for example). These are called compound nouns. Compound nouns can be written as one word (*headlight*, for example) or as two words (*traffic sign*, for example).

9 **A.** Put a word from column A with a word from column B to form compound nouns. You will need to use words from column A and column B more than once.

A	B
parking	limit
traffic	space
speed	jam
head	sign
stop	light
car	ticket
gas	lot
	crash
	station
	meter

Compound Nouns

1. parking space
2. ______________
3. ______________
4. ______________
5. ______________
6. ______________
7. ______________
8. ______________
9. ______________
10. ______________
11. ______________
12. ______________
13. ______________
14. ______________
15. ______________

B. Complete the following sentences with compound nouns from exercise 9A.

1. A ______________ can be fatal on the road.
2. No driver wants to get a ______________ .

3. Drivers must stop at a ____________________ .

4. A ____________________ often causes drivers to be late for work.

5. A ____________________ can be difficult to find in a busy part of town.

6. All drivers must sometimes go to a ____________________ .

7. You put money into a ____________________ .

8. A ____________________ can be red, green, or yellow.

9. Drivers should not go faster than the ____________________ .

10 With other students, talk about the following topics:

1. an accident you have been in or a serious accident you have seen
2. what annoys you most about other drivers on the road
3. a time you were stopped (or someone you were with was stopped) by the police

WORD STUDY

> **FOCUS ON THE GRAMMAR OF TWO-WORD VERBS:** Some two-word verbs can be separated. Other two-word verbs cannot be separated.

Two-word verbs consist of a verb and a preposition or of a verb and an adverb. The meaning of a two-word verb is often very different from the meanings of the two words taken separately.

I *turned on* the engine.
My car *broke down.*
Look out! A car is coming.
I *dropped off* my children at school.

Sometimes a two-word verb has no object; that is, it is intransitive.

My car *broke down* as I was driving home.
Look out!

Other times a two-word verb has an object. With these two-word verbs, you must be careful to put the object in the correct place.

Turn on your headlights.
I *ran into* a tree.

The object of many separable two-word verbs can be put in two places: after the verb or after the preposition/adverb.

Object
Turn the headlights *on*.

OR

Object
Turn on the headlights.

The object of inseparable two-word verbs can be put in only one place: after the preposition/adverb.

Object
The bus *ran into* the car.

[NOT: The bus ran the car into.]

11 **A.** A good dictionary will tell you the meaning of a two-word verb and where to put the object. Look at the following dictionary information.

drop (sbdy./sthg.) **off** **drop off** (sbdy./sthg.)	*v adv* [T] to leave (somebody or something) somewhere; leave a vehicle
get into sthg.	*v prep* [T] to enter (a vehicle)
pick (sbdy./sthg.) **up** **pick up** (sbdy./sthg.)	*v adv* [T] to arrange to go and get
run into sthg.	*v prep* [T] (of a vehicle) to meet (something) with force
run (sbdy./sthg.) **over** **run over** (sbdy./sthg.)	*v adv* [T] (of a vehicle and its driver) to knock down and pass over the top of
turn (sthg.) **off** **turn off** (sthg.)	*v adv* [T] to stop a flow of (water, gas, electricity, etc.)
turn off sthg.	*v adv* [I;T] to leave one road for another
turn (sthg.) **on** **turn on** (sthg.)	*v adv* [T] to cause (water, gas, electricity, etc.) to flow

B. Put the word in parentheses in the correct place to complete the sentence. If there are two correct answers, write both.

Example: Turn the headlights. (on)
Turn on the headlights. AND *Turn the headlights on.*

1. She got the taxi and left. (into)

____

2. Robert usually picks his wife at the subway station. (up)

____

3. The taxi driver dropped Dr. Norton at her office. (off)

____

4. How could you forget to turn the engine? (off)

____

5. The bus ran the dog. (over)

The bus ran over the dog.

6. We turned the highway at the first exit. (off)

We Turned off The highway

7. I can't believe you ran a police car! (into)

I can't believe you ran into a police car.

Sometimes the object is a pronoun like *it* or *them*. When the two-word verb is separable, these pronouns usually go *between* the verb and the preposition/adverb.

Turn ***them*** *on.* [NOT: Turn on them.]

When the two-word verb is inseparable, these pronouns go *after* the preposition/adverb.

The bus *ran into* ***it.***

12 Complete the following sentences with a two-word verb and a pronoun.

1. My driving teacher told me to turn on my turn signal, so I turned it on.
2. I didn't think I was going to run into the bicycles parked near the school, but I wasn't careful, so I ran into them.
3. My driving teacher told me to turn off the ignition, so I Turned.
4. My driving teacher told me to get into the car, so I got into.
5. My driving teacher picks up students at their homes. My lesson begins at 1:30, so today at 1:30 she picked me up.
6. My driving teacher drops off students at their homes, so today when my lesson was over, she droped me off

REVIEW 1

1 Some words have a positive meaning. For example, if you are in a good mood, you are happy. Therefore, *in a good mood* has a positive meaning. Other words have a negative meaning. For example, if you are in a bad mood, you probably are angry about something. Therefore, *in a bad mood* has a negative meaning. Finally, some words have a neutral meaning. They have neither a positive nor a negative meaning.

Do the following words have a positive, a negative, or a neutral meaning? Check (✔) the appropriate column. When you have finished, compare answers with another student. You may disagree, so be sure to give the reasons for your answers.

	Positive	**Negative**	**Neutral**
1. annoyed	______	______	______
2. blame	______	______	______
3. break down	______	______	______
4. concerned	______	______	______
5. do a favor	______	______	______
6. ease one's conscience	______	______	______
7. even-tempered	______	______	______
8. fatal	______	______	______
9. fault	______	______	______
10. fed up	______	______	______
11. grateful	______	______	______
12. irritated	______	______	______
13. moody	______	______	______
14. obligated	______	______	______
15. parking ticket	______	______	______
16. relieve	______	______	______
17. shatter	______	______	______
18. signal	______	______	______

2 How well do you know the derived forms of the words you studied in Units 1, 2, and 3? Read each dialogue. Complete the sentences with the correct form of the words in *italics*.

1. *argument*

   Amy: But Mom, Dad said it was okay for me to go and I want to go.

   Mom: Please don't argue________ with me. You can't go and that's that. Don't Talk back To Me!

2. *duty*

   A: He has always taken very good care of his parents.

   B: I know. He's a very Dutyful________ son.

3. *grateful*

   A: I don't know how to express my Gratitude________ for all you have done. Gratefulness.

   B: It was my pleasure. I'm glad I was able to help you.

4. *relieve*

   A: You must have been happy when the police found Tony.

   B: Oh, yes. I felt such great ________________ when I heard the news.

5. *moral*

   A: Stealing is Morally________ wrong.

   B: That's true, but would you call taking from the rich and giving to the poor stealing?

6. *sympathetic*

   A: I have no job right now and I won't be able to take care of my family if your bank doesn't lend me money.

   B: We Sympathize________ with your problem, but there's nothing we can do.

7. *sympathetic*

   A: Why don't you have any Sympathy________ for her?

   B: Because she does nothing to help herself. She wants others to solve all her problems for her.

8. *obligated*

   A: I don't understand why you have agreed to do something you don't want to do.

   B: Because I feel it is an obligation________. I would feel bad if I didn't do it.

3 Look at the words in the box below. If a friend asked you what they meant, how would you teach them to your friend? Would you show a picture? Give an example? Demonstrate the meaning? Give a definition?

Write each word from the box in the appropriate column below. When you have finished, compare lists with other students.

Example: A picture: *stop sign*—

An example: *vehicle*—a bus, a car, a truck
A demonstration: *slam*—stand up, go to the door, and slam it
A definition: *fatal*—causing death

grab	duty	moral	parking meter
argument	have no conscience	steer	maintain
can't stand	sympathetic	crash	traffic jam

Show a Picture	Give an Example	Demonstrate the Meaning	Give a Definition

Put into: put in. Put off = Pospone
Put down = Humilate.
Put on = Get dressed = Take off -

4 Read each dialogue. Complete the sentences with the following words:

down, into, off, over, through, up.

1. **A:** Could you pick me __up__ at the office?
   B: Sure. I'll come at five o'clock to get you.
2. **A:** Why are you speeding __up__? The sign says slow __down__.
   B: I know, but I want to pass the car on the right.
3. **A:** I can't put __up__ with this noise anymore. I'm leaving.
   B: No, don't leave. I'll get the kids to play more quietly.
4. **Taxi Driver:** Miss, where do you want me to drop you __off__?
   Customer: At the corner will be fine.
5. **A:** Look at the map. After we get on Route 93, where do we turn __off__?
   B: At Exit 34.
6. **A:** Why are you in a bad mood?
   B: Because I got a ticket for going __through__ a red light. But the light was yellow, not red.
7. **A:** What happened to your car?
   B: Someone ran __into__ it when it was parked in front of the bank.
8. **A:** Why is your little boy so sad?
   B: Because our dog died last week after a truck ran __over__ it.
9. **A:** Why are you late? Don't you know the meeting began ten minutes ago?
   B: Yeah, I know, but I couldn't help it. My car broke __down__.
10. **A:** Where are you going? I thought you had to study.
    B: I'm fed __up__ with studying all the time. I need a break. I'm going to the movies.

5 Rewrite each sentence using the words in parentheses. Do not change the meaning.

1. I'm tired of hearing all your complaints. *(fed up)*
   I'm fed up with hearing all your complaints.
2. She gets angry easily. *(temper)*
   ____

3. You didn't stop at the stop sign. *(go through)*

____

4. I didn't do anything wrong. *(fault)*

____

5. I feel great today. *(mood)*

____

6. He can't stop thinking about what he did to his friend. He feels terrible. *(conscience)*

____

7. I hate driving in the center of town. *(stand)*

____

8. I don't want to do it. *(mood)*

____

6 Play Tic-Tac-Toe in two teams. Team A is *X* and Team B is *O*. One player from Team A chooses a word and uses it in a sentence. If Team B agrees that Team A's sentence is correct, Team A puts an *X* on the word. Then a player from Team B takes a turn. The first team to have three *X*'s or three *O*'s in a straight line (—, |, \, or /) is the winner.

Game One

run into	furious	scream
slam	relieve	drop off
trunk	lose one's temper	back up

Game Two

hood	tempera-mental	speed-ometer
put up with	run over	pick up
go through	sharp curve	yell

7 Listen to the story.

Now listen to the story again. On a piece of paper, write down what the speaker says.

8 **A.** You have learned many words in the last three units. They are listed below.

Unit 1

annoyed
be in a mood
be in a bad mood
be in a good mood
be in the mood
blame
even-tempered
fault
fed up (be fed up)
furious
grab
have an argument
have a bad temper
have a hot temper
hot-tempered
lose one's temper
moody
put up with
scream
shatter
slam
stand (can't stand)
temperamental
yell

Unit 2

be on one's conscience
concerned
conscience
do a favor
duty
ease one's conscience
grateful
have a clear conscience
have a guilty conscience
have no conscience
irritated
moral
obligated (be obligated)
relieve
sympathetic

Unit 3

back up
break down
crash
drop off
fatal accident
go through
maintain
pick up
run into
run over
sharp curve
signal
slow down
speed up
steer
turn off
vehicle

B. It is difficult to remember and to use all of these words equally well. For example, some of the words you may be using already. Some of the words you may know the meaning of but are not comfortable using. Other words you may not remember at all. To help you check how well you know these words, write each of them in one of the following columns.

I Can Use These Words Correctly	I Know the Meaning of These Words, But I Can't Use Them Yet	I Think I Know the Meaning of These Words, But I'm Not Sure	I Don't Know These Words

UNIT 4

SICKNESS AND HEALTH

Do you know these words?

to avoid	to expose	to ease	virus
to catch	to infect	to get over	symptom
to spread			cure

PRESENTATION

1 Check (✔) *Usually, Never,* or *Sometimes* to describe how you feel when you have a cold. Compare answers with another student.

When I have a cold	Usually	Never	Sometimes
1. I have a headache.			
2. I have an earache.			
3. I have a stomachache.			
4. I have a toothache.			
5. I have a sore throat.			
6. I feel sick to my stomach.			
7. I get dizzy. Mareado			
8. I sneeze a lot.			
9. I cough a lot. Tos			
10. My back hurts. dolor			

When I have a cold	Usually	Never	Sometimes
11. My leg hurts.			
12. I have a stuffy nose.			
13. I have a runny nose.			
14. I have a fever.			

2 This unit's reading is an article about colds. How much do you know about colds? Write *T* if you think the statement is true. Write *F* if you think the statement is false.

1. To avoid colds, stay inside as much as possible during cold weather. ______

2. When you sneeze, cover your nose and mouth with your hand. ______

3. Chicken soup helps you feel better when you have a cold. ______

Read the text. Which statements in Exercise 2 are true according to the information in the text?

Listen as you read the article.

The Cold Facts

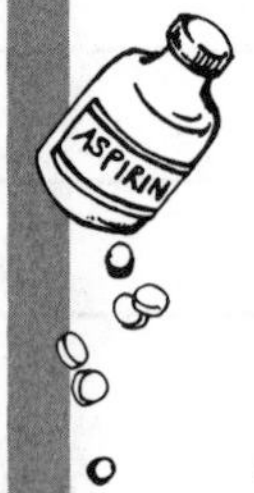

Winter is coming. It's time again for coughing and sneezing. You can't *avoid* colds completely. But by knowing more about how they're *caught* and *spread*, you can make your winter healthier. Here's a quiz to test your cold knowledge.

To *avoid* colds, stay inside as much as possible during cold weather.

False. Cold weather does not cause colds—*viruses* do. There are more than 100 different cold *viruses*. Children are more likely than adults to *catch* colds because they are *exposed* to more cold *viruses* in school.

When you sneeze, cover your nose and mouth with your hand.

False. This usually helps *spread* colds. When you sneeze, cold *viruses* are carried through the air and can *infect* other people around you. Colds may also be *spread* by indirect contact. A person who sneezes covers his mouth, touches an object (such as a glass or telephone), another person handles the object and then touches her mouth, nose, or eyes.

It's better to sneeze into a tissue and then throw the tissue away. If you don't have a tissue, sneeze into your sleeve, or turn your head toward the floor. Then wash your hands.

Chicken soup helps you feel better when you have a cold.

True. Studies have shown that hot drinks can relieve a stuffy nose. Liquids can also help relieve a dry throat, and aspirin will temporarily *ease* headaches and other aches and pains.

Although these methods often relieve cold *symptoms,* you won't *get over* a cold faster. Your body's natural defenses, along with time and rest, are the only known *cure,* but you can help prevent colds by eating lots of fruits and vegetables.

3 The following statements were made by worried parents. Check (✔) the statements that are correct.

1. "It's cold outside. If you go out, you'll catch a cold." ______
2. "You're worried about your daughter catching a cold? Well, if a lot of children at her school have a cold, maybe she should stay at home." ______
3. "You used your tissue only once. Keep it in your pocket and use it again." ______
4. "You don't have a tissue? Well, cover your nose and mouth and sneeze with your head toward the floor." ______
5. "Your sore throat will feel better if you have this soup." ______
6. "Your cold will go away faster if you take some aspirin." ______

> **FOCUS ON GUESSING MEANING:** You can often guess the meaning (or general meaning) of a word if you look for clues which come before and/or after it.

4 Look at the words in *italics* in the article on page 46 and in the sentences below. Try to guess the meanings of these words. Circle the correct answers.

1. You can *avoid* getting fat if you don't eat too much and you exercise often.
   To *avoid* means to
   a. do something about.
   b. keep away from.
2. If you *catch* a cold on Monday, you will still have the cold on Tuesday.
   To *catch* means to
   a. get.
   b. have.
3. The illness *spread* throughout the town. Many people became ill.
   To *spread* means to
   a. leave an area.
   b. move over an area.
4. You may get the *virus* if you are with people who already have it.
   A *virus* is a very small living thing which
   a. goes from one person's body to another and causes illness.
   b. cannot be seen but may live on food or dirt.

5. Children are *exposed* to more cold viruses in a classroom than they are at home.

   Exposed means leave unprotected

   a. unprotected from.
   b. safe from.

6. If one child at school has the illness, she can *infect* many other children. Then, they too will have to go to the doctor.

   To *infect* means to

   a. put disease into the body of someone.
   b. touch someone.

7. Take some aspirin. It will help to *ease* the pain.

   To *ease* means to make pain

   a. worse.
   b. less.

8. A sore throat and a runny nose are *symptoms* of a cold.

   A *symptom* is a

   a. sign that you have an illness.
   b. sign that you are getting better.

9. When you *get over* a cold, you feel fine.

   To *get over* means to

   a. become ill again after an illness.
   b. become healthy again after an illness.

10. There is no *cure* for the disease yet, but scientists are looking for one. However, a doctor can give you something to help you feel a little better.

    To bring

    A *cure* is

    a. a way of making someone healthy when they are ill.
    b. medicine to give someone when they are ill.

5 Complete the following sentences. When you have finished, compare answers with another student.

1. In my country, one of the ways people avoid catching colds is by drinking orange juice, Taking Vitamins.
2. In my country, people think the best way to get over a cold is by drinking milk and Honey.
3. The last time I caught a cold was ________________.
4. The AIDS virus is not spread by ________________.
5. Children should not be exposed to ________________.

always you use by all The verbs you need Ing ej: By exercising

6. To ease the pain caused by a backache, I ______________________.

7. A dog can infect you if ______________________.

8. You can get food poisoning from eating old chicken. One of the symptoms of food poisoning is ______________________.

9. I hope that one day there will be a cure for ______________________.

EXPANSION

FOCUS ON COLLOCATIONS: Some words are used together frequently. For example, we talk about a ***bad** cold*. We do not say a ***big** cold*.

6 **A.** Study the words in the diagram which are often used with *headache, cold, pain, ill,* and *illness.*

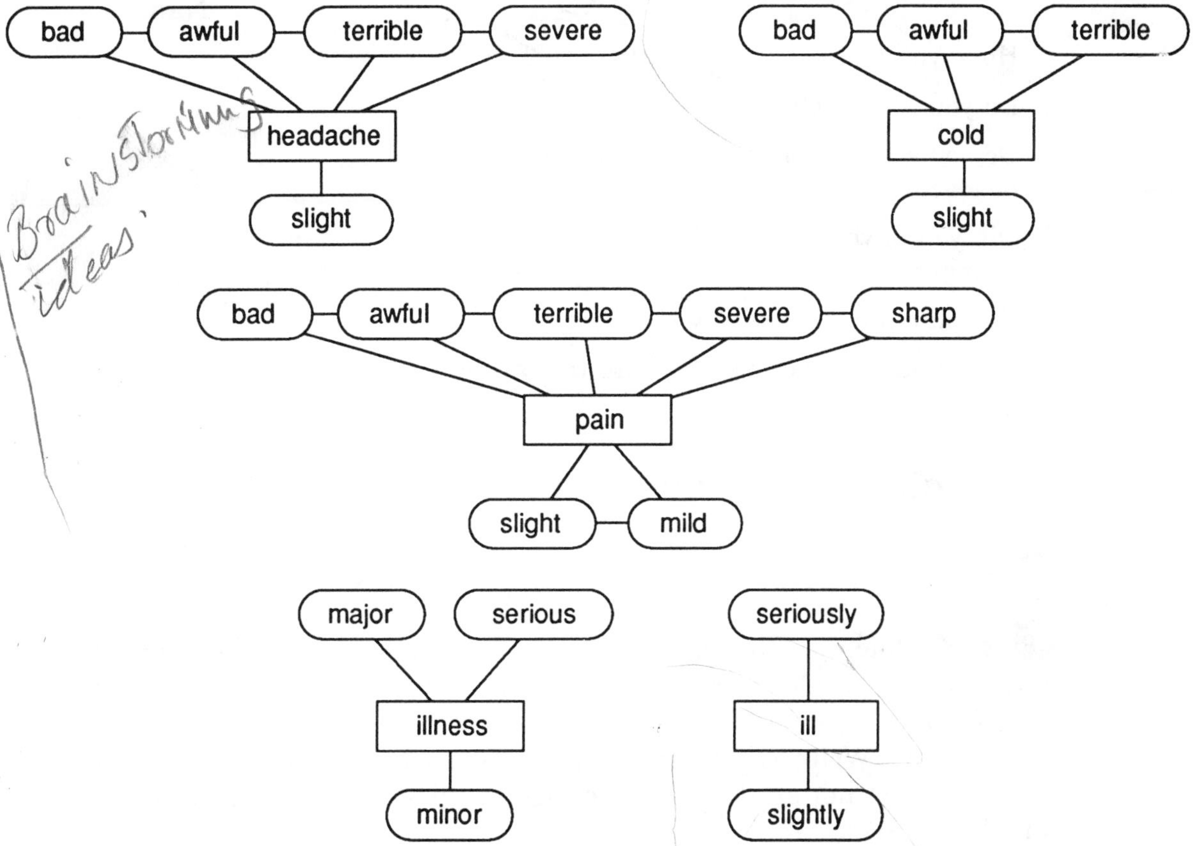

B. Write the opposites of the words in *italics*. (Note: There can be more than one correct answer.)

1. a *terrible* pain in my back: ______________________
2. a *slight* headache: ______________________
3. a *minor* illness: ______________________
4. a *slight* cold: ______________________
5. a *terrible* headache: ______________________
6. a *serious* illness: ______________________
7. a *bad* cold: ______________________
8. a *mild* pain: ______________________
9. *seriously* ill: ______________________

C. Walk around the class and ask other students the following questions. When someone answers yes, write that person's name in the blank. Then ask your own questions to get more information.

	Name
1. Have you had an awful cold recently?	____________
2. Do you have a slight headache right now?	____________
3. Do you stay in bed when you have a severe headache?	____________
4. Did you have a serious illness when you were younger?	____________
5. Do you often feel slightly ill before a test?	____________
6. Have you ever had a sharp pain in your back?	____________

FOCUS ON TOPIC-RELATED WORDS: It helps to remember words related to the same topic.

7 **A.** Following are words for some common health problems. Check with another student or use your dictionary to find the meaning of any words you don't know. Which problems are serious and which are usually not serious? Write the words in the appropriate column. Then compare lists with another student. If there are any differences, explain the reason for your answer.

if you have a sore feet:
I soak my feet in hot water.

influenza (*or* the flu)	a stroke	constipation
indigestion	AIDS	a rash
diabetes	cancer	high blood pressure
a heart attack	diarrhea	a cold

Serious	**Usually Not Serious**
	a rash.
	a cold
	diarrhea.
	indigestion
	constipation
	influen

B. What other words for health problems do you know in English? Add them to the appropriate column above.

8 Number the following events in the order in which they usually happen.

a. You cure an illness. 5

b. You ease the pain caused by an illness. 4

c. You get an illness. 1

d. You get over an illness. 6

e. You have an illness. 2

f. You treat an illness. 3

9 **A.** Study these charts. The first chart shows the differences in meaning among the verbs on the top. The second shows the differences in use.

	cure	treat	ease	relieve	get over
to give medicine, for example, to *try* to make symptoms go away		✓			
to become better with or without help from a doctor or from medicine					✓
to bring back to good health with medicine and other help from doctors	✓				
to cause pain to become less, but not to go away			✓		
to free from pain				✓	

	cure	treat	ease	relieve	get over
a person	✓	✓			
a serious illness	✓	✓			?*
a minor illness	?*	✓			✓
symptoms		✓		✓	
a pain		✓	✓	✓	✓
an infection	✓	✓			

*Some people use this expression; others think it is incorrect.

B. Which nouns in the box can be used with the following verbs? Write the appropropriate nouns next to the verbs. Then compare lists with other students.

a cold	cancer
a headache	AIDS
a heart attack	diabetes
high blood pressure	the flu
a backache	a stroke

1. ease: a headache, a backache
2. avoid: high blood pressure
3. catch: a cold, The flu
4. cure: 6 - 8
5. get: 1 2 . 4 5 6 7 8 9
6. get over: The flu 1.2 - 5 - 9.
7. have:
8. relieve: diabetes 2 - 5.
9. treat: AIDS

FOCUS ON DERIVED FORMS: When you learn a new word, it is useful to learn the other forms related to that word: the derived words.

10 **A.** Write the derived forms of the words in *italics*. (Use a dictionary if you need help and be sure to check the pronunciation of the derived words.)

Verb	Noun	Adjective
to avoid	1. avoidance	2. avoidable
to expose	3. exponser	
to infect	4. *an* infections	5. infectious
to spread	6. Spread	
to treat	7. *a* Treatmaint	8. Treatable
9. To cure.	*a cure*	10. careful
	a pain	11. painful

B. Use words from exercise 10A to fill in the crossword puzzle.

Across

3. If he'd been more careful, the accident wouldn't have happened. It was __________.
5. The __________ for cancer can include drugs.
7. Her headache was so __________ that she couldn't work.

Down

1. Cholera is now a __________ disease.
2. They are trying to control the __________ of the disease before many others become ill.
4. AIDS is an __________ disease.
6. If you want to stay well, avoid __________ to infections.

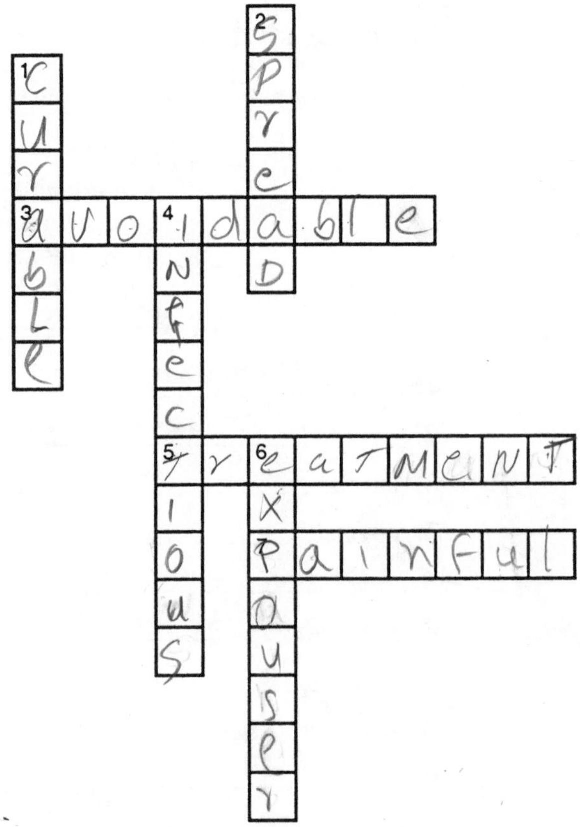

11 Work in three groups: Team A, Team B, and Team C. Team A writes down the condition part of five sentences; these sentences must all begin with *If* and must be on the topic of health. Team A then reads out each of its conditions. Team B must complete each sentence by using a word from this unit. Team C decides if Team B's answers are correct. The groups then switch. The team gets one point for each correct answer. The team with the most points is the winner.

Example: Team A: "If you take aspirin,"
Team B: "you can relieve a headache."
Team C: "Correct!"

WORD STUDY

> **FOCUS ON THE GRAMMAR OF WORDS:** Dictionaries have important grammar information to help you use new words correctly.

Unit 1 explains some of the information a dictionary will tell you. (If you don't remember this information, look back at page 10.)

A dictionary will also tell you if a verb is followed by a gerund [+ *v-ing*] or by an infinitive [+ *to-v*].

12 **A.** The following words appear in the unit. Study the grammar information which comes before each definition.

a·void *v* [T +*v-ing*] to miss or keep away from, esp. on purpose
catch *v* **caught, catching** [T] to get (an illness); become infected with
cure *v* **cured, curing** [T] to make (a disease, illness, etc.) go away, esp. by medical treatment
ex·pose *v* **-posed, -posing** [T *to*] to uncover; leave unprotected
in·fect *v* [T *with*] to put disease into the body of (someone)
spread *v* **spread, spreading** [I;T *out*] to (cause to) open, reach, or stretch out; make or become longer, broader, wider, etc.

B. The sentences on page 56 in column A are correct. The sentences in column B are not correct. In each blank write the grammar information from the dictionary entry which shows why each sentence in column B is wrong.

Example: re·lieve *v* **-lieved, -lieving** [T] to lessen (pain or trouble)

A	B	
If you have a headache, aspirin will relieve it.	If you have a headache, aspirin will relieve.	[T]

(*Relieve* is transitive [T], so it must have an object. *Relieve* has no object in the sentence in column B.)

	A	B	
1.	Everyone wants to avoid getting sick.	Everyone wants to avoid to get sick.	______
2.	I caught a cold on the weekend and I still have it.	I catched a cold on the weekend, and I still have it.	______
3.	Doctors can cure it.	Doctors can cure.	______
4.	Being around sick people exposes you to many viruses.	Being around sick people exposes you with many viruses.	______
5.	If you are infected with this virus, you need to see a doctor immediately.	If you are infected by this virus, you need to see a doctor immediately.	______
6.	In the sixteenth century, some diseases spread all over Europe.	In the sixteenth century, some diseases spreaded all over Europe.	______

FOCUS ON SOUND–SPELLING DIFFERENCES: In English, words with a similar spelling are often pronounced differently. You can use your dictionary to find out how to say a word correctly.

Study these examples: *ea* in *spr**ea**d* is pronounced /ɛ/ as in *bed,* but *ea* in ***ea**se* is pronounced /iʸ/ as in *meat; i* in *v**i**rus* is pronounced /aɪ/ as in *I'm,* but *i* in *d**i**sease* is pronounced /ɪ/ as in *sit.*

13 **A.** Look at the pronunciation of the following words. Write each word in the appropriate column.

dead /dɛd/	disease /dɪˈziʸz/	ease /iʸz/	treat /triʸt/
headache /ˈhɛdeʸk/	spread /sprɛd/	health /hɛlθ/	heal /hiʸl/
earache /ˈiəreʸk/	breath /brɛθ/	breathe /briʸð/	

ea sounds like ***bed***	*ea* sounds like ***meat***
spread	ease

B. Now look at these words and write them in the appropriate column.

diabetes /ˌdaɪəˈbiʸtɪs/	diarrhea /ˌdaɪəˈriʸə/	diet /ˈdaɪət/
disease /dɪˈziʸz/	dizzy /ˈdɪziʸ/	examine /ɪgˈzæmɪn/
medical /ˈmɛdɪkəl/	prescribe /prɪˈskraɪb/	prescription /prɪˈskrɪpʃən/
sick /sɪk/	virus /ˈvaɪrəs/	

i sounds like ***I'm***	*i* sounds like *s**i**t*
virus	disease

UNIT 5

RELATIONSHIPS

Do you know these words?

to influence	reliable	companion	loneliness
to turn to	emotional	state	benefit
to treat		behavior	

PRESENTATION

1 Below are some kinds of animals which people keep as pets. Circle the animals which you think make good pets. Cross out the animals which you think make bad pets. Explain your reasons to another student.

a cat	a dog	fish	a frog	a parrot
a rabbit	a snake	a turtle	white mice	

2 How much do you know about pets? Write *T* if you think the statement is true. Write *F* if you think the statement is false.

1. A pet can help people who are seriously ill feel better. ______

2. The elderly often feel happier when they have a pet. ______

3. Prisoners who have pets cause fewer problems. ______

Read the text. Which statements in Exercise 2 are true according to the information in the text?

Listen as you read the article.

Influence of Pets Reaches New High

If an animal can possibly be a pet, someone in the United States is probably living with it, making money from it, or studying its effect on people. Today 61 percent of American families own animals.

Pets are important not only to people's mental health but to their physical well-being, too. According to researchers who have studied the relationship between humans and animals, pets can *influence* heart rate and blood pressure. They can provide people in wheelchairs with social contact that is frequently more *reliable* than contact with human *companions* is. They can also improve the *emotional state* and *behavior* of prisoners and the elderly.

People are *turning to* pets more often these days for several reasons. Big-city life leads to a *loneliness* that animals often fulfill. Psychologists suggest that many Americans are recognizing the *benefits* of pet *companionship* and are *turning to* them to fill the emptiness in their lives. "Pets are a part of the family," said one psychologist. "We *treat* our pets as if they were human beings."

According to one survey, 99 percent of dog and cat owners say they talk to their pets. Forty percent of the people asked also said they kept pictures of their pets in their wallets and celebrated their pets' birthdays.

3 Check (✓) the correct column. Did the article talk about:

	Yes	No
1. which animals make the best pets?	______	______
2. how many people in the United States have pets?	______	______
3. why people are turning to pets for companionship?	______	______
4. some ways in which pets help people?	______	______
5. why children love animals?	______	______

4 Ask another student these questions.

1. Do you have a pet? If so, what kind of animal is it? Do you think of your pet as your companion?
2. Do you know any people who treat their pet like a part of their family? What exactly do they do? Do you think people should treat animals in this way?
3. In what way can an animal be a more reliable companion than a human being?
4. What are the benefits of giving a pet to a child?

> **FOCUS ON GUESSING MEANING:** You can often guess the meaning (or general meaning) of a word if you look for clues which come before and/or after it.

5 **A.** Read the sentences and guess the meanings of the word in *italics*. Write a definition, synonym, or translation for each word in *italics*. (If you write down a translation, check a bilingual dictionary to see if you guessed correctly.)

1. Pets can *influence* heart rate and blood pressure. They can also cause a change in the way prisoners behave.

   influence: ______________________________

2. Peggy is a *reliable* person. If she says she will do something, you can be sure she'll do it.

   reliable: ______________________________

3. You need a *companion,* someone to do things with, because you spend too much time alone.

   companion: ______________________________

4. Think before you make a decision. Whether you love it or hate it is not important right now. This is just an *emotional* reason, and deciding to do something just because you have strong feelings about it can be a mistake.

   emotional: ______________________________

5. Ever since his cat died, he's been in a terrible *state.* He's never happy, and his physical condition isn't very good either. He's been sick a lot.

   state: ______________________________

6. Your *behavior* at the party made me very angry. The way you acted was embarrassing.

   behavior: ______________________________

7. Whenever I have a problem, I *turn to* my best friend. I can go to her and ask for her help anytime I need to.

   turn to: ______________________________

8. Not all people who live alone suffer from *loneliness*. However, people who are lonely need to make a special effort to talk to others and find things to do. In this way, they won't be unhappy.

   loneliness: ______________________________

9. There are good reasons to have a dog. If you live alone, one of the *benefits* is that you feel safer. However, having a dog also has disadvantages, such as having to take it out for walks.

   benefit: ______________________________

10. My husband and I *treat* our pets as if they were human beings. We talk to them, and many of the things other people do with their children, like playing ball, we do with our pets.

   treat: ______________________________

B. Write down the parts of each sentence in exercise 5A which helped you guess the meaning of the word in *italics*.

1. influence: ______________________________
2. reliable: ______________________________
3. companion: ______________________________
4. emotional: ______________________________
5. state: ______________________________
6. behavior: ______________________________
7. turn to: ______________________________
8. loneliness: ______________________________
9. benefit: ______________________________
10. treat: ______________________________

6 ROLE PLAY: In this role play, one person will be Student A and the other will be Student B. Read the situation. After you have read the situation, read the information for your role. (Note: Do not read each other's roles.)

Situation

Huntington Memorial Hospital in California uses dogs as "therapists" for cancer patients. The dogs wear photo identity cards and scarves with the name of the hospital. A current study shows that patients who are visited by these therapy dogs have lower blood pressure rates. It is also believed that the patients are in better moods when they are with these pets.

Roles

Student A: You have been informed that you must put your 85-year-old aunt in the hospital for a long time. You've heard about Huntington's program. Your aunt has always liked dogs, and you feel very strongly that she should have visits from a therapy dog. You must convince the director of the hospital, Student B, of the benefits of this program.

Student B: You are the director of a hospital. You are sympathetic to the idea that pets are helpful companions, but you do not believe animals should be in hospitals. You must convince Student A that allowing dogs into a hospital would cause too many problems.

EXPANSION

> **FOCUS ON WORD GROUPS:** Sometimes it helps to remember words which are connected to the same idea.

7 **A.** There are different kinds of relationships people have with others. Study the words in the following "relationships" tree.

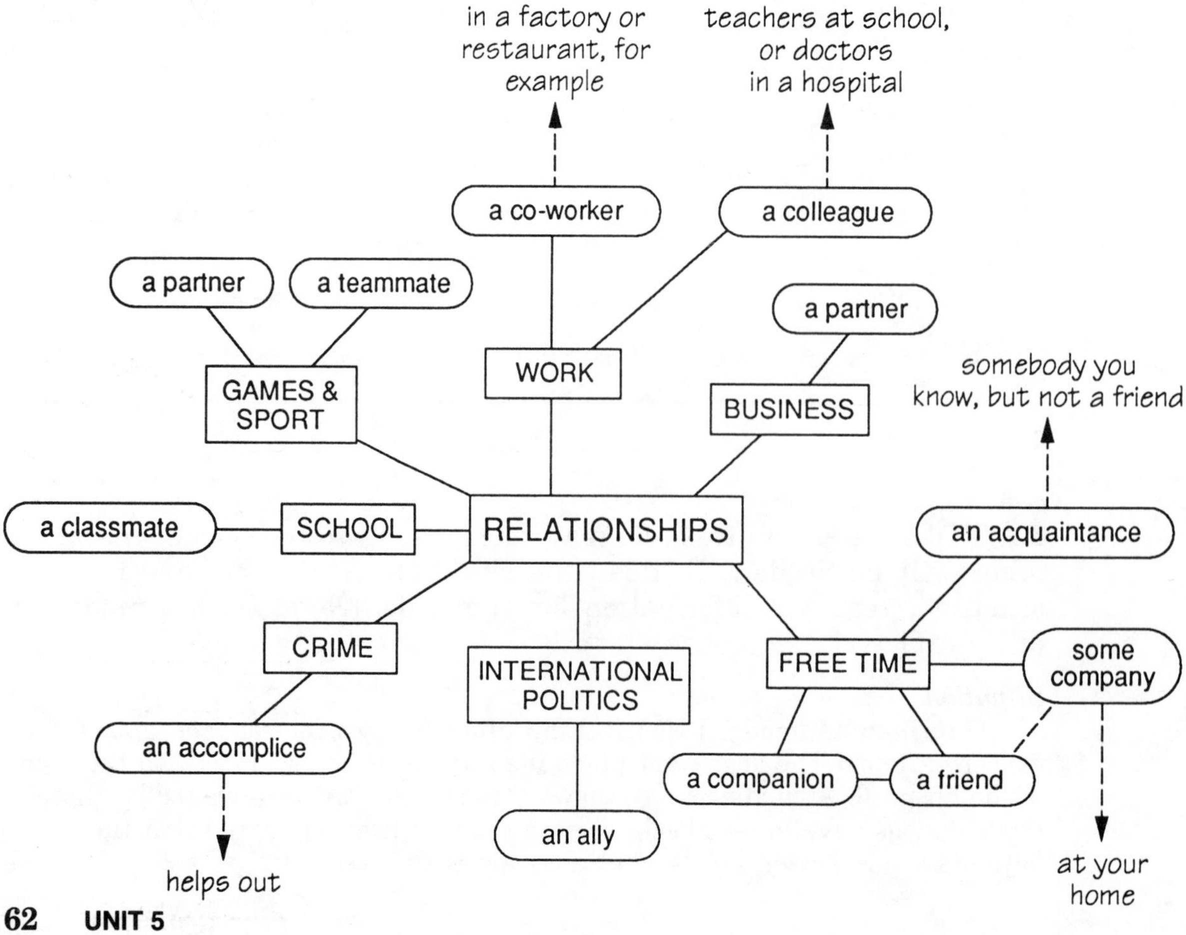

B. To whom are these people probably speaking? Use the words in exercise 7A to fill in the blanks. (Note: You can use any words from 7A except *friend.*)

Example: "Good game! Do you want to play tennis again next weekend?" To a tennis partner.

1. "In war or peace, we are together." ______________________
2. "Can you help me move these boxes? The boss wants all of them on the truck." ______________________
3. "Did you do the homework for today?" ______________________
4. "Would you like some tea?" ______________________
5. "Danny, throw the ball to me." ______________________
6. "Hello. It's nice to see you again." ______________________
7. "Lynn, can I talk to you for a minute about one of your students, Luis Rivera? He's in one of my classes, too." ______________________
8. "Hurry up and start the car. The police will be here any minute. Do you want to end up in jail?" ______________________

> **FOCUS ON DERIVED FORMS:** When you learn a new word, it is useful to learn the other forms related to that word: the derived words.

8 Write the derived forms of the words in *italics*. (Use a dictionary if you need help and be sure to check the pronunciation of the derived words.)

Noun	Verb	Adjective
behavior	1. behave	
benefit	2. __________	3. __________
loneliness		4. __________
influence	*influence*	5. __________
6. __________	*treat*	
7. __________		*emotional*
8. __________	9. __________	*reliable*

FOCUS ON SUFFIXES: A suffix is a group of letters added to the end of a word. The suffixes *-ship* and *-ness* mean "state of" and can be added to many adjectives and nouns to form new nouns.

adjective	+ *-ness*	
lonely	+ *-ness*	= loneliness (the state of being lonely)
noun	+ *-ship*	
companion	+ *-ship*	= companionship (the state of having or being a companion)

9 **A.** Look at the following list of words. Look up any words you do not know in the dictionary. Then make new words by adding *-ship* or *-ness*. Be sure to check the spelling of these new words.

1. companion	companionship	**7.** friendly	______
2. lonely	loneliness	**8.** friend	______
3. partner	______	**9.** selfish	______
4. leader	______	**10.** relation	______
5. kind	______	**11.** thoughtful	______
6. sad	______	**12.** lazy	______

B. On a separate sheet of paper, make a list of other nouns you know which end in *-ship* and *-ness*. Then compare lists with another student. Are there any more words to add to your list?

10 Answer these questions. Share your answers with your classmates.

1. What do you think makes a good friendship?
2. How would you rate your relationship with your parents: very good, good, not very good? With your brothers and sisters? With your teacher?
3. Do you think it is best to get married for love or for companionship?
4. When you think of the following characteristics, which of your relatives and friends come to mind: kindness, thoughtfulness, laziness, friendliness, selfishness?

FOCUS ON PROVERBS: Proverbs are short, well-known sayings. There are many proverbs in English with animal words.

11 **A.** Match the proverbs in column A with their meanings in column B.

A

1. You can't teach an old dog new tricks.
2. When the cat's away, the mice will play.
3. Her bark is worse than her bite.
4. Birds of a feather flock together.
5. You can lead a horse to water, but you can't make it drink.

B

a. You can try to force people to do what you want them to do, but they will only do it if they want to.
b. If you have been doing something one way for a long time, it's difficult to change.
c. This person says she will do something to hurt you, but in the end she will do nothing.
d. Students, for example, do what they are not supposed to do when the teacher isn't in the classroom.
e. People prefer the company of others who are just like them.

B. Now think of situations in which you might use the proverbs in exercise 11A.

12 Talk in groups of three or four students. Discuss the different topics on page 66 according to the different letters in your first and/or last name. For example, a person named Al Ray would talk about the subjects in boxes 1, 8, 11, and 15, because the letters of his first and last name are next to these boxes. Which subjects will you talk about? Turn to page 66 and look at the boxes next to the letters in your first and/or last name. Then talk about your subjects with the other members of your group.

A	[1] why companionship is important
B or C	[2] which makes a better pet, a cat or a dog
D	[3] what should be done to people who treat animals badly
E or F	[4] a time when you were treated badly
G or H	[5] who you turn to when you have a problem
I	[6] what you do when you feel lonely
J or K	[7] your emotional state at the moment
L or M	[8] what is needed for a successful relationship with members of the opposite sex

N	[9] a reliable person you know
O or P	[10] a person who has had an influence in your life.
Q, R, or S	[11] the typical behavior of a puppy
T	[12] a classmate you know well
U or V	[13] besides being pets, how dogs and cats are beneficial to humans
W or X	[14] two people who are famous partners
Y or Z	[15] why countries become allies

WORD STUDY

FOCUS ON CHOOSING THE CORRECT MEANING: One word in English can have many meanings. Therefore, it is important when using a dictionary to scan, to look at quickly without careful reading, all of the definitions for a word. Then decide which definition is the one you want.

13 Read the following sentences. Then scan the dictionary entries on page 67 for *state* and *treat*. For each sentence write the number of one correct definition of *state* or *treat*.

1. Chicago is in the *state* of Illinois. ______
2. Pets can improve the emotional *state* of prisoners and the elderly. ______
3. In many countries, telephone companies are owned and run by the *state*. ______
4. I hope you don't mind if I *treat* you to dinner. ______
5. They *treat* their dog as if it were a person. ______
6. He is being *treated* for his illness at a Miami hospital. ______

state *n* **1** [C] a condition in which a person or a thing is: *the state of one's health* | *a happy state of mind* **2** [C;U] a country or its government: *Should industry be controlled by the state?* **3** [A;U] the formality and ceremony connected with high-level government: *the President's state visit to Britain* **4** [C] any of the smaller partly self-governing parts making up certain nations: *the 50 states of the US*

treat *v* **1** to act or behave towards: *She treats us like children.* **2** to deal with; handle; consider: *This glass must be treated with care.* **3** to try to cure by medical means: *to treat a disease* **4** to buy or give (someone) something special: *I'm going to treat myself to a vacation in the mountains.*

FOCUS ON THE MEANING OF STEMS: Many English words have been formed with parts (or stems) of Latin and Greek words. A stem is the main part of a word. If you know the meaning of the stem, you can often guess the general meaning of a word which contains it.

14 **A.** Look at the following definitions for words which contain the stem *bene.* Guess the meaning of *bene* and write it in the blank.

beneficent *adj fml* doing good; kind
benefit *n* advantage; profit; good effect
benevolent *adj* having or expressing a wish to do good

bene: ____________________

B. The stem *fac* means "to do, to make"; the stem *dict* means "to say, to speak." Look at the definitions on the right. Which is the definition of *benediction* and which is the definition of *benefactor*? Write the correct word in each blank.

1. ____________________: a person who does good or who gives money to an organization, for example, in order to help others
2. ____________________: a blessing

UNIT 6

LOVE AND MARRIAGE

Do you know these words?

a couple	romantic	to break up	to get along
a proposal	stable	to go out with	to fall in love
respect			to be attracted to

PRESENTATION

1 Discuss marriage in your culture.

- At what age do most women get married? What about men?
- Are parents involved in helping their children find a husband or wife? How?
- Is marriage considered important in your culture? Why?
- In the traditional American wedding, the bride wears a white gown. What does the bride wear in a traditional ceremony in your country? What does the groom wear?
- What happens before the wedding ceremony? What happens during the ceremony? What happens at the celebration after the ceremony?

2 You are going to read an interview in which an American anthropologist talks about marriage in African and American cultures. The following words are in the interview.

wedding	satisfactory	long-term	relationship	expect
spouse	is supposed to do	qualities	partner	divorce

a. Circle the words which you think generally refer only to marriage.
b. Cross out any words which you think people would never use to talk about marriage.
c. Compare answers with another student.

3 Check (✔) the statements you agree with. Discuss your answers with another student.

1. There must be love for a marriage to be successful. ______

2. Love is not important for a marriage to be successful. ______

3. For a marriage to be successful, husbands and wives must do what their spouse expects. ______

4. There is a difference between a good marriage and a successful marriage. ______

Read the interview. Then decide which of the statements the speaker would probably agree with.

Listen as you read the interview.

Does Romantic Love Work?

Q You say that so many *couples* in America *break up* because of the importance we give to *romantic* love. How is our view of love different from that of others?

A We've taken the kind of love that humans learn from their mothers and added romance to it. We think about love as soon as we start *going out with* someone. We can't imagine marriage *proposals* or weddings as events that have little to do with love. As a result, the importance we give to being in love makes it difficult for us to see that we can have a perfectly satisfactory long-term relationship without it.

Q So you're saying relationships are more *stable* in other cultures because they don't have *romantic* love?

A Absolutely. There's got to be *respect* and you've got to be able to *get along*. There's also got to be an ability to see the other person for what he or she is. But you don't have to have "love" to do it well.

The Africans I lived with expected the person they married to be a "good spouse." And if you ask what a good spouse is, you'll be told the same thing by everybody. The women say, "He gives me enough cloth. He gives me enough land to put a farm on." The men say, "She works hard on the farm. She cooks when she's supposed to." But he doesn't have to listen to her troubles. And she doesn't have to worry if he's happy.

Q So what's the problem with love?

A If you decide who to marry based on *romantic* love, you may not see the real qualities of the other person. You give your partner qualities that aren't really there. Then, once you realize the person you *were attracted to* and *fell in love* with isn't who you thought he was, he's a rat.

Q Does the high divorce rate worry you?

A No, I'm surprised there aren't more divorces. There was never a time when most marriages were good. We have more good marriages now than ever before. We are open about so many things. And we're not so ashamed when things go badly.

4 Discuss the answers to the following questions.

1. Look back at your answers to exercise 3. Has the interview you have just read changed any of your opinions? Which ones? How have your opinions changed?
2. Look at lines 16 through 22 again. Do you completely agree, partially agree, or completely disagree with the African definition of a good spouse?
3. Do you agree that when people fall in love they give their partner "qualities that aren't really there"? Give examples to support your opinion.

> **FOCUS ON GUESSING MEANING:** You can often guess the meaning (or general meaning) of a word if you look for clues which come before and/or after it and if you use the knowledge you have about the world around you.

5 **A.** Look at the words in *italics* in the interview again and try to get a general understanding of their meaning. Then use the phrases in the box to complete the statements which follow. These statements, when complete, will provide you with an explanation of the meaning of each word in *italics*.

> **a.** begin to love someone very much
> **b.** spend time together on a regular basis
> **c.** have a friendly relationship
> **d.** does not change easily and is long-lasting
> **e.** there is something about them that you like and that pulls you toward them
> **f.** about love
> **g.** their relationship is ended
> **h.** asking her to get married
> **i.** have a good opinion of them
> **j.** are usually married, live together, or are on a date

1. People who *get along* with each other have a friendly relationship.
2. If two people are a *couple,* they ______________________.
3. If a woman thinks about a man's *proposal,* she thinks about his ______________________.
4. When you *fall in love,* you ______________________.
5. When two people are *going out,* they are usually of the opposite sex and they ______________________.
6. When two people *break up,* ______________________.
7. A *romantic* movie is a movie ______________________.

8. If you have *respect* for your parents, you ______________________.

9. A relationship is *stable* when it ______________________.

10. When you *are attracted to* people, ______________________.

B. Refer back to the meaning of the words in exercise 5A and complete the following statements. When you are finished, compare answers with another student.

1. When I fall in love, ______________________.
2. I'm attracted to people ______________________.
3. I won't go out with anyone who ______________________.
4. A relationship is no longer stable when ______________________.
5. What I respect most about my best friend is ______________________.
6. I don't get along with ______________________.
7. When two people become a couple, ______________________.
8. For me, a romantic evening includes ______________________.
9. Most marriages break up because ______________________.
10. Many women accept a man's proposal because ______________________.

6 **A.** In groups of four to six students, make up a story. The first person uses one of the words below to begin the story. The next person must use another word to continue the story, and so on. Every person in the group must use a different word to make up a part of the story. The story is finished when it has a logical end and when all the words have been used.

couple	romantic	proposal	respect	be attracted to
break up	go out with	stable	get along	fall in love

B. Individually, write your group's story and add as many details as you can. When you are finished, compare your final version of the story with the versions of the other group members.

EXPANSION

FOCUS ON TWO-WORD VERBS: In English there are many common verbs with two parts. The meaning of a two-word verb is often very different from the meaning of the two words taken separately. For example, to *break up* means to "end a relationship."

7 **A.** Look up the following two-word verbs in your dictionary. Find the meaning of the verbs when they describe love or relationships.

ask (someone) out	fall for	go with
make up	split up	stand (someone) up

B. Choose the most appropriate response that B would make to A's statement. Write the response in the blank.

a. That wasn't nice of him.
b. But don't you know he's married?
c. Why? I thought you were so happy together.
d. That's good. You two make such a nice couple.
e. Where are you going to go?
f. Really? I didn't know that.

1. **A:** I fell for Eric the moment I saw him.
   B: But don't you know he's married?
2. **A:** Tommy has asked me out.
   B: ________________
3. **A:** Laurie and I had a big fight last week, but we've made up.
   B: ________________
4. **A:** Karen is going with Bill.
   B: ________________
5. **A:** Sam and I have split up.
   B: ________________
6. **A:** David stood me up last night.
   B: ________________

FOCUS ON COMMONLY CONFUSED EXPRESSIONS: Expressions related in meaning are often confused.

8 **A.** The expressions in the boxes on page 74 are easily confused. The sentences in the bubbles show these expressions in use. Try to understand the difference in their meaning and then write your answer to each question.

1. | love someone   be in love with someone |

I'm in love with you. I can't live another day without you.

Who would most probably say, "I'm in love with you": a mother to her child, a brother to his brother, or a boyfriend to his girlfriend? ____________________

2. | date someone   have a date with someone |

Shelley is dating Vince. They met three months ago.

Linda has a date with Greg tonight.

Which couple spends time together frequently? ____________________

3. | go with   go out with |

Barbara has been going with Paul for two years.

Amy has been going out with Jim for two years.

I'm going out with some friends tonight.

Sue is going out with Bill tomorrow.

a. Which expression always means "over a period of time"? ____________________

b. Which expression can mean "over a period of time" or "one time"? ____________________

c. Which expression always means "have a relationship with someone of the opposite sex"? ____________________

4. | be seeing* someone   go out on a date with |

Did you know that Andrea is seeing Charlie?

Did you hear that Carol is going out on a date with Ted tomorrow?

a. Which couple spends time together frequently? ____________________

b. Is the expression *be seeing someone* similar in meaning to *date someone* or to *have a date with someone*? ____________________

*When the verb *see* has this meaning, it occurs in *-ing* form.

5. | separate   break up OR split up |

Richard and Sandy have separated.
Are they getting a divorce?
I hear that Joe and Helen are breaking up.
Tim and Judy split up two years ago.

a. Joe and Helen and Tim and Judy could be husband and wife or boyfriend and girlfriend. What is the relationship between Richard and Sandy? ______________

b. Does *separate* mean the same as *be divorced*? ______________

B. Write the answers to the following questions in the blanks. When you have finished, compare answers with another student.

1. How are *"I love you"* and *"I'm in love with you"* different in meaning?

____

____

2. How are *date* and *have a date* different in meaning?

____

____

3. How are *go with* and *go out with* similar in meaning?

____

____

4. How are *go with* and *go out with* different in meaning?

____

____

5. How are *separate* and *break up* (or *split up*) different in meaning?

____

____

9 Put the following events in the order in which they usually occur.

a. They get engaged. ______
b. They fall in love. ______
c. They are attracted to each other. ______
d. They start seeing each other again. ______
e. They go out. ______
f. They go together for a year. ______
g. He asks her out. ______
h. They make up. ______
i. Two people meet. 1
j. They get divorced. ______
k. They get married. ______
l. They separate. ______
m. They break up. ______
n. He proposes. ______

10 Make a list of the qualities you think a good wife has and the qualities you think a good husband has. Then compare your list with other students.

A Good Wife	A Good Husband

11 **A.** Read the following letter written to the advice column of a newspaper. In groups of four to six students, talk about and take notes on the ways of solving the problem. Then talk to someone from another group. Did both your groups come up with similar ways of solving the problem?

> **Dear Aggie:** I've been going out with the same woman for four years. I'm very much in love with her and she says she loves me. But every time I want to discuss the subject of marriage, she says she is not "the marrying kind." Maybe she's just afraid because her parents got divorced when she was young.
>
> Although I'm always happy when I'm with her, I'm not happy that she can't promise me a stable relationship in the future. I don't know how much longer I can go on like this. What do you think I should do?—**Don't Know What to Do**

B. Read the following responses to letters written to the advice column of a newspaper. In your group, discuss what you think "Confused" and "Worried" wrote in their letters. Then write one of the letters. When you have finished, compare letters with other students.

Dear Confused: You should wait. When you're not sure about something, it's best to take your time and think things over carefully.

Dear Worried: Someone who makes dates and breaks them doesn't have much respect for other people. There may be some good reasons why you've fallen for this person, but if you are looking for stability in a partner, it isn't likely you'll find it with this one.

WORD STUDY

FOCUS ON THE GRAMMAR OF WORDS: Dictionaries have important grammar information to help you use new words correctly.

12 **A.** Study the dictionary entry for *propose*. Pay particular attention to the different grammar patterns that are used after *propose*. Notice that the meaning changes according to the grammar pattern.

pro·pose *v* **1** [T + *v-ing*/(*that*)] to suggest: *I propose resting for half an hour.* | *I propose that we take a rest.* **2** [T + *to-v*] to intend: *I propose to go to Washington on Tuesday.* **3** [I;T *to*] to make an offer of (marriage) (to someone)

B. Read the sentences and pay attention to the grammar patterns after *propose*. Use this grammar information to find the correct definition. Write the number of the correct definition in each blank.

1. Did you hear that Jay *proposed* last night? ______
2. The president *proposes* meeting the visitors next Monday. ______
3. We *propose* that you provide us with more information before you ask us to make a decision. ______
4. We *propose* to meet again in a month's time. ______

FOCUS ON DERIVED FORMS: There can be more than one adjective or noun derived from, for example, a verb. Therefore, when looking up derived forms, be sure you find the derived form which is related in meaning to the word you have just learned.

13 Scan the dictionary entries of the two nouns derived from the verb *propose* and the two adjectives derived from the noun *respect*. Then complete the sentences which follow with one of the derived words.

pro·pos·al /prə'poʷzəl/ *n* **1** [+*to-v/at/for, often pl*] a plan or suggestion: *peace proposals* **2** [*of*] an offer of marriage **3** [+*to-v/that/of*] the act of proposing: *the proposal that we should rest for a while*

prop·o·si·tion /ˌprɑpə'zɪʃən/ *n* **1** [+*that*] a statement in which an opinion or judgment is expressed **2** a suggested business offer or arrangement: *He* ***made me a proposition*** *concerning the sale of my car.*

1. I haven't decided whether to accept Steven's ____________________ . I'm just not sure I'm ready for marriage.
2. The ____________________ by the President that all is well in the country is mistaken.
3. His ____________________ to improve the schools is an interesting one.

re·spect·a·ble /rɪ'spɛktəbəl/ *adj* **1** showing or having standards acceptable to society: *It's not respectable to be drunk in the street.* | *to put on a clean shirt and look respectable*

re·spect·ful /rɪ'spɛktfəl/ *adj* [*to*] feeling or showing admiration or honor: *The crowd waited in respectful silence for the President to speak.*—opposite **disrespectful**

4. When you go to a job interview, you should look ____________________ .
5. Children should be ____________________ to older people.

14 **A.** Look up the verb *relate* in your dictionary. How many nouns are derived from *relate*? List these nouns on the line below.

____

B. Now complete these sentences with nouns derived from *relate*.

1. My ____________________ all live in different parts of the country. I have an aunt and uncle in California, some cousins in Texas, and my parents are in Virginia.
2. I have a good ____________________ with my brothers and sisters.
3. ____________________ between the two countries are not good.

REVIEW 2

1 Some words have a positive meaning. For example, people who are in love are usually very happy. Therefore, *in love* has a positive meaning. Other words have a negative meaning. For example, someone who has a heart attack is very ill and probably has to spend time in the hospital. Therefore, *heart attack* has a negative meaning. Finally, some words have a neutral meaning. They have neither a positive nor a negative meaning.

Do the following words have a positive, a negative, or a neutral meaning? Check (✓) the appropriate column. When you have finished, compare answers with another student. You may disagree, so be sure to give the reasons for your answers.

	Positive	Negative	Neutral
1. accomplice	______	______	______
2. ally	______	______	______
3. attracted to	______	______	______
4. break up	______	______	______
5. colleague	______	______	______
6. couple	______	______	______
7. cure	______	______	______
8. ease	______	______	______
9. get over	______	______	______
10. go out with	______	______	______
11. influence	______	______	______
12. loneliness	______	______	______
13. sharp pain	______	______	______
14. slight cold	______	______	______
15. stable	______	______	______
16. stand someone up	______	______	______
17. symptom	______	______	______
18. turn to	______	______	______

2 How well do you know the derived forms of the words you studied in Units 4, 5, and 6? Read each dialogue. Complete the sentences with the correct form of the words in *italics*.

1. *avoid*

   A: The whole problem was ____________________ . Why didn't you do something?

   B: I know. I feel so bad.

2. *cure*

   Patient: Doctor, is the disease ____________________ ?

   Doctor: Oh, yes. Don't worry. But you must take this medicine for the next two months.

3. *expose*

   A: Why are you putting cream on your face and arms?

   B: Because ____________________ to the sun can be dangerous.

4. *infect*

   A: Look at this cut on my hand.

   B: It doesn't look good. Put something on it. You could get an ____________________ .

5. *spread*

   A: I don't think the school is doing enough to prevent the ____________________ of the disease.

   B: Madam, I promise you we are doing all we can.

6. *treat*

   Patient: Doctor, where will I have to go for this ____________________ ?

   Doctor: We'll be able to take care of you at the local hospital.

7. *companion*

   A: What do you think most people want from marriage?

   B: Some people marry for money, but I think most want ____________________ .

8. *benefit*

   A: Don't you know that exercise is ____________________ to your health?

   B: Of course I know that, but who has the time to run and swim? I'm a very busy person.

9. *reliable*

A: I think we should buy this car. It's such a nice-looking car.

B: But, dear, ____________________ is much more important. You don't want a car that breaks down all the time, do you? I think we should buy the other one.

10. *reliable*

A: Who do you think I should get to do the job?

B: Dave. You can always ____________________ on him to do good work.

11. *influence*

A: Who has been the most ____________________ person in your life?

B: My mother.

12. *behavior*

Father: I don't like the way you ____________________ at the party.

Sandy: But, Dad, it wasn't my fault.

3 Look at the following words. What year in your life do you associate with each of the words? Write the year in the blanks. When you have finished, explain to another student what happened to you that year.

Example: severe pain 1990
I had a severe pain in the heel of my foot in the fall of 1990. It was so bad I tried not to walk too much. After two months of treatment, the pain went away.

1. major illness	__________	**7.** proposal	__________
2. classmate	__________	**8.** fall in love	__________
3. emotional state	__________	**9.** behavior	__________
4. loneliness	__________	**10.** virus	__________
5. split up	__________	**11.** respect	__________
6. romantic	__________	**12.** influence	__________

4 Read each dialogue. Complete the sentences with the following words: *along, for, out, over, to, up, with.*

1. **A:** Who do you turn __________ when you have a problem?

   B: My best friend. He's always there for me when I need help.

2. **A:** You've been going __________ Charlie for a long time. Aren't you going to get married?

   B: No, we like our relationship just the way it is.

3. **A:** I heard you and Donna had a big fight. Are you still angry with each other?

   B: Oh, no. We made __________ a couple of days ago.

4. **A:** Stan stood me __________ again last night. This is the second time in the past month he has let me wait around all evening for him.

   B: You must be furious.

5. **A:** Why has Gemma been in such a bad mood lately?

   B: Because she and her boyfriend broke __________ a couple of weeks ago.

6. **A:** Could you take care of the baby for me tonight if I bring her over to your place?

   B: I don't think that would be a good idea. Ari still hasn't gotten __________ his cold. The baby could catch it.

7. **A:** When did you realize you were in love?

   B: I fell __________ Eliza the moment I saw her. It was love at first sight.

8. **A:** How are you and your new boss getting __________?

   B: Oh, fine. I really like her.

9. **A:** I asked Bernadette __________ and she said yes.

   B: Where are you going to go, to the movies or to a restaurant?

5 Use the grammar information given with each dictionary entry and decide which sentences below are correct. Circle the correct answers.

acquaintance [C] a person whom one knows, esp. through work or business, but who may not be a friend

company [U] one or more guests

get over [T] to return to one's usual state of health, happiness, etc., after a bad experience of or with

make up [I] to become friends again after (an argument)

respect [U *for*] admiration; feeling of honor

stroke [C] a sudden illness in part of the brain which can cause loss of movement in parts of the body

1. **a.** I was talking to acquaintance of mine from school.
   b. I was talking to an acquaintance of mine from school.

2. I'm sorry, Adam. I can't talk on the phone right now.
   a. I have company.
   b. I have a company.

3. a. I'm sure you feel terrible, but you'll get over.
b. I'm sure you feel terrible, but you'll get over it.

4. a. I want you boys to stop fighting and make up.
b. I want you boys to stop fighting and make up it.

5. a. We have great respect for her.
b. We have great respect by her.

6. a. Our neighbor has had stroke and is in the hospital.
b. Our neighbor has had a stroke and is in the hospital.

6 Play the Word and Topic Game. Get into groups of four or five. You will need to have a die (or six pieces of paper with the numbers 1 to 6 written on them). One student in the group throws the die (or picks a piece of paper) and moves the correct number of squares on the board. The students must use the word on this square in a sentence. Then, he or she throws the die again (or picks another piece of paper). This number is for the topic. The student must then use the word in a sentence about this topic. If the other players think the sentence is logical, the first player gets a point. Then it is the next person's turn. The player with the most points at the end of the game is the winner. (Time limit: 20 minutes)

Example: 2 (catch), 3 (driving)
I caught an awful cold last week. When I was driving the other day, I was sneezing so much that I didn't see the car in front of me suddenly stop, and I ran right into it.

Topics

1. Anger
2. Right and Wrong
3. Driving
4. Sickness and Health
5. Relationships
6. Love and Marriage

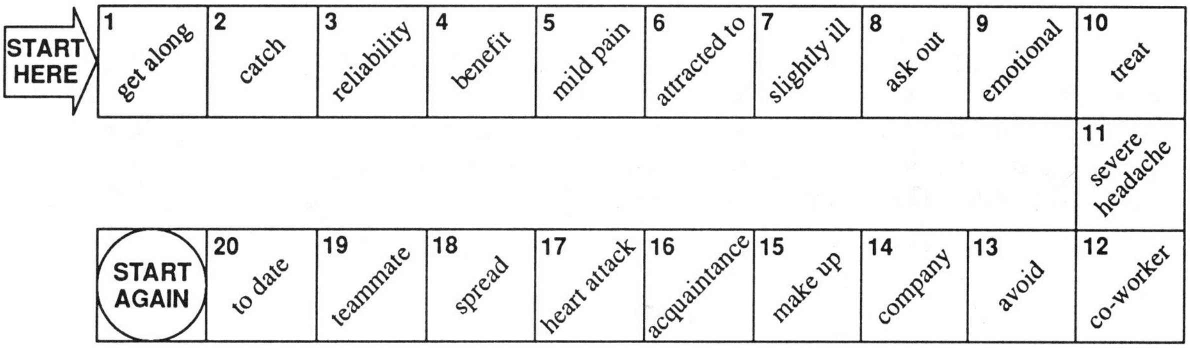

7 Listen to the story.

Now listen to the story again. On a piece of paper, write down what the speaker says.

8 **A.** You have learned many words in the last three units. They are listed below.

Unit 4	Unit 5	Unit 6
avoid	accomplice	ask out
bad cold	acquaintance	attracted to (be attracted to)
cancer	ally	break up
catch	behavior	couple
cure	benefit	date (*v*)
diabetes	classmate	fall for
ease	colleague	fall in love
expose	companion	get along
get over	company	go out with
heart attack	co-worker	go with
high blood pressure	emotional	in love (be in love)
infect	influence	make up
major illness	loneliness	proposal
mild pain	partner	respect
minor illness	reliable	romantic
serious illness	state	see (be seeing someone)
severe headache	teammate	separate
sharp pain	treat	split up
slight headache	turn to	stable
slightly ill		stand someone up
spread (*v*)		
stroke		
symptom		
treat		
virus		

B. It is difficult to remember and to use all of these words equally well. For example, some of the words you may be using already. Some of the words you may know the meaning of but are not comfortable using. Other words you may not remember at all. To help you check how well you know these words, write each of them in one of the following columns.

I Can Use These Words Correctly	I Know the Meaning of These Words, But I Can't Use Them Yet	I Think I Know the Meaning of These Words, But I'm Not Sure	I Don't Know These Words

C. You have probably found when learning new vocabulary that you do not always remember the same words after you have studied them. Words you think you know one week you can't remember at all the next week. Or this week you find yourself using words that last week you thought you didn't know. Look back at your columns of words on page 44. Move any words you want to a different column. (From time to time, check your lists and move any words you want to a different column.)

UNIT 7 POLITICS AND PROTEST

Do you know these words?

a campaign	an issue	a party	eligible	to oppose
a candidate	a majority	a right	qualified	
an election				

PRESENTATION

1 People decide who to vote for for different reasons. Put the reasons below in order from the most important for you (write 1) to the least important (write 10). (Add any other reasons that are important to you.) Then compare answers with other students.

I vote for a politician

a. who has a good personality. ______

b. who is married and has a happy family life. ______

c. whose ideas I agree with. ______

d. who has a good education. ______

e. who has no health problems. ______

f. who has worked in government before. ______

g. who is religious. ______

h. who has specialized knowledge. ______

i. who I think will be a strong leader. ______

j. who is honest. ______

other reasons ______________________________

____

AMERICAN LANGUAGE COMMUNICATION CENTER
PENNSYLVANIA HOTEL
7th Ave. Between W.32st. & W.33st.
NEW YORK, NY 10001
TEL: 1-800-ENGLISH

PAYMENT NO.: 1/0000038263

DATE: 12/13/96 TIME: 10:23:05
CARD#: PAYMENT TYPE: CASH

Book	QNTT	Total
READING & VOCAB. LEVEL(TX)	1	20.00

Sub Total -> 18.48
Tax -> 1.52
Total -> 20.00

* AMOUNT PAID: $ 20.00 * THANK YOU

OPERATOR: SARA FITZROY

SIGNATURE________________

2 The chart has been filled in with the American and British systems of government. Fill in the boxes on the right with the system of government in your country.

	American	British	My Country
Leader	President	(Country) Queen or King (Government) Prime Minister	
Lawmakers	Congress	Parliament	

3 The subject of this unit's editorial is how people become members of Congress. Read the article. Then circle the correct answer below.

The writer wants

a. American citizens to continue to vote for members of Congress.
b. the President of the United States to choose members of Congress.
c. to choose members of Congress from a list of all voters.

Listen as you read the article.

EDITORIAL

End Elections

I suggest that there be no more congressional *elections*. Instead, members of Congress should be selected by lottery. The current system doesn't work because most voters are forced to choose between two *candidates* they don't want. Also, 83 percent of congressional elections are won by the *candidate* who spends the most money during the *campaign*—making promises, visiting local fairs, expressing ideas in ads.

The *majority* of the members of Congress are rich, white males. Half of them are lawyers and another third are businessmen. Some may say that lawyers and businessmen are the most *qualified* people in our society to make laws, but I disagree. It should be the role of lawyers to write laws, not make them. Likewise, successful businessmen may be good at making a profit in private life, but they have not stopped the country from going a trillion dollars into debt.

Some who *oppose* this suggestion may say that the average citizen does not have the specialized knowledge needed to make decisions about important *issues*. But not very many of our present members of Congress from either *party* are *qualified* to handle these *issues* either.

In the new system I am suggesting, people would be chosen to be a congressperson from a list of *eligible* voters. These people would be required to pass a test on the Constitution.[1] Those who did not would then receive six weeks of instruction. Anyone who did not pass a second time would lose the *right* to be a member of Congress.

I realize that there would be many problems during the change to a nonelected Congress, but I believe that in time such a system would succeed.

[1] Constitution: ideas on which laws of the land are based

4 Check (✔) the statements with which you think the writer would agree.

1. The present system of electing people to Congress is not a good one. ______
2. Americans have too many choices when they vote for a member of Congress. ______
3. Mostly rich candidates become members of Congress. ______
4. There are not enough women in today's Congress. ______

5. A person with a college education is more qualified to be a member of Congress than a person without an education. ______

6. Members of Congress do their job well. ______

FOCUS ON GUESSING MEANING: When you read, it is important to try to guess the meaning (or general meaning) of new words from the context.

5 Look at the words in *italics* in the editorial. Try to guess their meaning from the way they are used. Circle the correct answers.

1. In an *election,* people __________ .
   a. vote
   b. make laws
2. A *campaign* takes place __________ people vote.
   a. after
   b. before
3. A *candidate* is a person who __________ an election.
   a. wins
   b. wants to win
4. If a *majority* of the people vote for you, you will have __________ of the vote.
   a. 49 percent
   b. 51 percent
5. A person who is *qualified* __________ special knowledge, skills, and experience for a job.
   a. has
   b. does not have
6. If you *oppose* an idea, you __________ with it.
   a. agree
   b. do not agree
7. *Issues* are __________ .
   a. people who discuss their ideas about politics.
   b. especially important subjects for discussion.
8. A *party* is __________ .
   a. a person who wants to be the leader of a country.
   b. a group of people with the same political ideas.
9. If you are *eligible* to vote, you are __________ to vote.
   a. allowed
   b. not allowed
10. In a democracy, people have the *right* to say whether or not they agree; that is, they __________ always give their opinion.
    a. can
    b. cannot

6 Check (✔) the statements which are true about politics in your country. Discuss your answers with another student.

1. Candidates in the last election were from two parties. ______
2. Most of the candidates in the last election were rich businessmen or lawyers. ______
3. The candidate who spent the most money during the campaign won the election. ______
4. An important issue in my country is equal rights for women. ______
5. Men and women over the age of 21 are eligible to vote in my country. ______
6. A majority of the people in my country oppose higher taxes. ______
7. The election system in my country should be changed. ______

EXPANSION

> **FOCUS ON SUFFIXES:** A suffix is a group of letters added to the end of a word. The suffix *-ism* often means "a set of ideas." The suffix *-ist* often means "someone who believes in that set of ideas."

7 **A.** Use your dictionary or check with another student to find the meaning of the words below. Also, mark the stressed syllable of each word and be sure you can say the words correctly.

capitalism	environmentalism	nationalism	sexism
communism	feminism	racism	terrorism

B. Now use the words in exercise 7A to answer the following questions. Remember to change the suffix. (Note: You will need to use one of the words in 7A twice.) What do you call:

1. a group of people of the same nationality who want independence from the country in which they are living? ________________
2. a person who believes that women should have the same rights as men? ________________

3. a person who believes that men are able to do most things better than women? ____________

4. people who believe that they are better than others because of their skin color? ____________

5. people who try to get what they want politically by using violence? ____________

6. people who think their country is better than all other countries? ____________

7. people who want to protect trees, animals, etc.? ____________

8. a person who agrees with the political beliefs of Lenin and Mao Tse-tung? ____________

9. people who believe that individuals should own property? They do not want the government to own property or control the money individuals make. ____________

8 Working with one or two other students, organize the words from exercise 7A into meaningful groups. You must decide how many groups there are, and you must give each category a name. Then compare answers with other groups.

> **FOCUS ON TOPIC-RELATED WORDS:** It helps to remember words related to the same topic.

9 **A.** Read the following article.

> **Marchers Oppose Government**
>
> At a demonstration in the capital yesterday, 10,000 people protested the government's decision not to ban the cutting down of trees in several national forests.

Which word from exercise 7A describes the 10,000 people mentioned in the article? Write your answer in the blank. environmentalists

B. Match each underlined word in exercise in 9A with one of the following definitions. Write the correct word in each blank.

1. be against something oppose
2. forbid ban - something
3. people who walk together in large groups to express their opinion Marchers
4. say strongly that you do not agree with something Protest.
5. event where a large number of people get together to show they do not agree with something Demostration.

> **FOCUS ON DERIVED FORMS:** When you learn a new word, it is useful to learn the other forms related to that word: the derived words.

10 Write the derived forms of the words in *italics*. (Use a dictionary if you need help and be sure to check the pronunciation of the derived words.)

Noun	Noun (the Person)	Verb	Adjective
1. a Vote	2. a voter	*to vote*	
3. opposition	4. an opponen	*to oppose*	
5. a Protest	6. a Protester	*to protest*	
a campaign	Campaigner	7. to Campain	
a demonstration	8. a demostrater	9. to Demostrate	
an election		10. to elect	
a government	Governer	11. to Govern.	
12. a March	*a marcher*	13. to March	
14. a Politecs	*a politician*		15. Political
16. eligibility			*eligible*
17. a equalification		18. to qualify	*qualified*

11 Write each of the following words somewhere on the map. Then explain to another student why you wrote the words in these places.

Example: I wrote *eligible* here because this is my country and I am eligible to vote there.
OR
I wrote *eligible* here because I want to study at a university in this country, and I hope I'll be eligible for a scholarship.

demonstration	environmentalist	majority	parties	racism
election	equal rights	march	protest	sexism
eligible	issue	opposition	qualified	terrorist

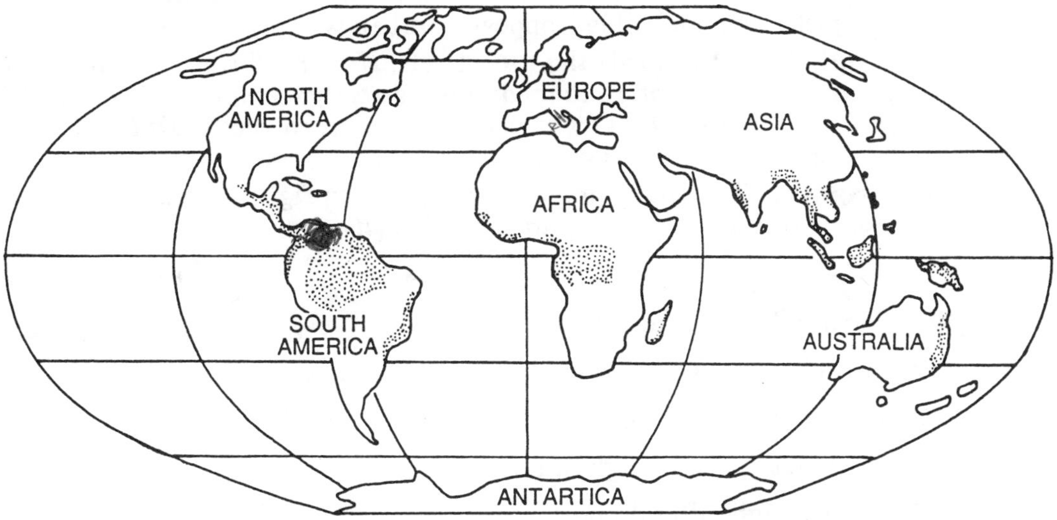

WORD STUDY

> **FOCUS ON CHOOSING THE CORRECT MEANING:** One word in English can be a noun, verb, adjective, and adverb and not change its spelling. One word can also have more than one meaning. It is important to learn to recognize and use the correct meaning.

12 There are six separate dictionary entries with the spelling *right.* Two of the entries are for the adjective, two are for the noun, one is for the adverb, and one is for the verb. Scan the six entries. Then write the number of the correct entry and the correct definition in the blanks following each sentence on page 94.

right[1] /raɪt/ *adj* **1** [A] on or belonging to the side of the body that does not contain the heart: *Most people write with their right hand.* **2** [A] on, by, or in the direction of this side: *a right turn*—opposite **left**

right[2] *n* **1** [U] the RIGHT[1] (1) side or direction: *Take the second turn on the right.* **2** [C] the right hand: *Hit him with your right.* **3** [U] (*often cap.*) political parties or groups that favor fewer political changes and less state control, and generally support business or those in official positions rather than the workers: *The right opposes the new taxes.*—compare LEFT[2]

right[3] *adj* **1** [F + *to-v*] just; morally good: *It's not right to tell lies.* **2** correct; true: *Is that the right time?*—opposite **wrong**

right[4] *n* **1** [U] what is RIGHT[3] (1): *She's old enough to know the difference between right and wrong.* **2** [S:U *of, to*] (a) morally just or lawful claim: *She has a right to half the money.* **3 in the right** having justice on one's side—opposite **in the wrong**

right[5] *adv* **1** towards the RIGHT[2] (1): *He turned right.*—opposite **left** **2** [*adv* + *adv/prep*] immediately; directly; completely: *Go right back to the beginning;* | *right now* **3** properly; correctly: *Did I do it right?*—opposite **wrong**

right[6] *v* [T] to put (something) right or upright again: *The car righted itself during the fall and landed on its feet.*

	Entry	Definition
1. Turn right at the next corner.	5	1
2. Seventeen-year-olds do not have the right to vote.		
3. Politicians on the right are opposed to the new law.		
4. He didn't know the right answer.		
5. I'll do it right after dinner.		
6. It's not right to take something that isn't yours.		

> **FOCUS ON PREFIXES:** A number of prefixes in English have the meaning "not" or "the opposite of." Some of these are *dis-, in-, non-,* and *un-*.

13 **A.** Look at the words below. Put a circle around the words which are in the editorial on page 88.

agree	disagree	eligible	ineligible
qualified	unqualified	elected	nonelected

B. Write the opposites of the words below in the correct column.

agree	educated	experienced	profit
approve	elected	honest	qualified
complete	eligible	member	successful

dis-	*in-*	*non-*	*un-*
disagree Disapprove Dishonest Disqualified	incomplete inoli		unqualified

C. Do the crossword puzzle using the words you wrote in exercise 13B.

Across

2. The results of the election are ___________ because not all the votes are in.
8. If people ___________ of a politician's way of life, they will not vote for him or her.
9. Anyone under age 35 is ___________ to be President of the United States.
10. ___________ organizations do not pay taxes because they do not make money.
11. ___________ people do not usually get the best jobs.

Down

1. Politicians from opposing parties often ___________ with each other.
3. It is difficult for ___________ politicians to win elections.
4. ___________ are not allowed in the meeting. It is for members only.
5. The candidate who was ___________ got only 20 percent of the vote.
6. Some Americans think that a person who knows little American history is ___________ to be in Congress.
7. Kings are ___________ leaders.
8. Many people think politicians are ___________.

UNIT 8

STUDYING

Do you know these words?

to fail	to drop	confused	complicated
to make sense	to require	brilliant	simple
to sign up		academic	

PRESENTATION

1 Look at the list of high school subjects. Cross out any subjects which you did not study. Add to the list any subjects not included which you studied in high school. Was studying these subjects a good experience or a bad one? Check (✔) the appropriate column. Compare experiences with another student.

	A Good Experience	A Bad Experience
A foreign language	______	______
Algebra	______	______
Biology	______	______
Calculus	______	______
Chemistry	______	______
Geography	______	______
Geometry	______	______
History	______	______
Literature	______	______
Physical education	______	______
Physics	______	______
Religion	______	______

2 In this unit's reading, a well-known American newspaper writer, Russell Baker, talks about how he decided to become a writer while he was in college. Below are eleven words from the reading. Check with another student or use your dictionary to find the meaning of any words which are new. Write *U* next to the word if people usually use it when talking about university life. Write *N* if people usually use it when talking about newspaper work. Write *BOTH* if people use the word to talk about university life and newspaper work.

1. professor __U__	**5.** campus ______	**9.** freshman ______
2. newspaper __N__	**6.** course ______	**10.** editors ______
3. write __BOTH__	**7.** schedule ______	**11.** story ______
4. lecture ______	**8.** scholarship ______	

3 Read the story. Then decide what advice the writer would probably give if he were talking to college students. Circle the correct answer.

a. It's important to decide what kind of work you want to do in the future and what you are going to study *before* you start college.

b. Keep an open mind. Don't decide what kind of work you are going to do in the future until you find something you really like doing at college.

Listen as you read the story.

Physics, Calculus—How I Became a Journalist

On my first day at Johns Hopkins University, I was listening to Professor Murnaghan lecture on differential calculus. This was a frightening experience because, after my first ten minutes in the course, I knew I was going to *fail.*

From the first day in calculus, I did not understand a thing Professor Murnaghan was trying to teach. Physics left me equally *confused.* Dr. Hubbard, the physics professor, was said to be just as *brilliant* as Dr. Murnaghan was, and I believed it, because I was completely lost in physics from his very first lecture. Nothing *made sense* in either course. Before the week was out, I knew I was going to *fail* physics just as surely as I was going to *fail* calculus.

By my third week on campus, I knew *signing up* for physics and calculus had been a terrible mistake. I could *drop* both courses, but doing so would leave my *academic* schedule full of free time. That was dangerous. The university had given me a full scholarship for the freshman year on the understanding that renewal for a second year would *require* a good *academic* record. Without that scholarship, I would have to quit college.

I was walking across the campus worrying about all this one sunny summer afternoon when I saw Charlie Sussman.

"Where you headed, Suss?"

On his way to learn newspaper writing, he said. He'd seen a notice on a bulletin board. The editors of the *News-letter,* the campus newspaper, were going to give an hour talk on newswriting techniques. The session was open to anyone. Why didn't I go with him?

Being unable to think about anything except physics and calculus, I said I wasn't interested.

"Oh, come on," he said. "What else do you have to do?"

A good question. The answer was, "Nothing."

He led the way to a small room with a couch and a few chairs. A half dozen other students came in and sat down. Then came two older, worldly-looking men who took chairs facing us and announced that they were editors of the *News-letter,* and one started talking about how to write a news story.

"The first thing to understand is the Four W's . . ."

I listened with interest. Compared to physics and calculus, writing a news story didn't seem *complicated* at all. All you had to learn was Who, What, Where, and When, then write a sentence containing that information, and you were writing a newspaper story. It seemed *simple.* It certainly seemed like more fun than calculus and physics. I decided I might give it a try.

4 What do you think probably happened next to the writer? Check (✓) the correct answers.

1. He decided to take another calculus course. ______
2. He decided to take another physics course. ______
3. He decided to take a writing course. ______
4. He got a job with the campus newspaper. ______

5 Ask another student these questions.

1. What kind of work do you (or do you hope to) do? What made you decide to do this kind of work?
2. How do you think the writer's life might have been different if he had not met his friend Charlie Sussman when he was walking across campus?
3. Has an unexpected meeting with somebody ever changed your life? Whom did you meet? How did this meeting change what you were planning to do?

> **FOCUS ON GUESSING MEANING:** You can often guess the meaning (or general meaning) of a word if you look for clues which come before and/or after it.

6 **A.** Read the sentences and guess the meaning of the words in *italics*. Write a definition, synonym, or translation for each italicized word. (If you write down a translation, check a bilingual dictionary to see if you guessed correctly.)

1. Calculus is very difficult. I don't understand a thing. What will I do if I *fail* next week's test? I'll be happy if I get a 70. A 70 out of 100 is not very good, but at least I'll pass the test.

fail: ______________________________

2. I'm very *confused* about this answer to the homework. I don't understand why my answer is wrong. Could you explain it to me?

confused: ______________________________

3. Justin is smart, but Paula is *brilliant*. It's rare to have a student who is so intelligent.

brilliant: ______________________________

4. What you've written doesn't *make sense.* I understand the meaning of the first sentence, but I don't understand the second at all. Could you explain what you are trying to say?

make sense: ______________________________

5. If you want to take the course with Professor Deevers, you should *sign up* now. The sign-up paper is on her door. Her course is very popular and she takes only fifty students. If you wait much longer, you probably won't be able to take it.

sign up: ______________________________

6. I hated the course and I didn't think I was going to do well, so I *dropped* it after two weeks. I feel much better now that I'm not taking it anymore.

drop: ______________________________

7. I went to an *academic* high school. The school prepared students to go to college, but there were also typing and driving classes for students who wanted to take them.

academic: ______________________________

8. You're *required* to take calculus, but you don't have to take physics.

require: ______________________________

9. This math problem is *complicated.* I don't usually find math difficult, but this problem has several parts to it and it will take me time to find the answer.

complicated: ______________________________

10. You may think this math problem is *simple* because it has only one part. However, I don't think it's so easy.

simple: ______________________________

B. Write down the parts of each sentence in exercise 6A which helped you guess the meaning of the word in *italics.*

1. fail: ______________________________
2. confused: ______________________________
3. brilliant: ______________________________
4. make sense: ______________________________
5. sign up: ______________________________
6. drop: ______________________________
7. academic: ______________________________
8. require: ______________________________
9. complicated: ______________________________
10. simple: ______________________________

FOCUS ON SYNONYMS: Some words may be similar in meaning. However, this does not mean that they have exactly the same meaning or that they can be used in exactly the same way.

7 Look at the pairs of words and phrases in the boxes. How are they similar? How are they different? Write the correct words in the blanks.

1. | failed   didn't do well |

a. Jennifer ____________________ on the test, but she passed. The passing grade was 65 and she got a 68.

b. Louis ____________________ the test. He got a 62.

2. | brilliant   intelligent |

a. Which word describes many university students? ________________

b. Which word describes people like Albert Einstein? ________________

3. | sign up   register |

a. You can't just sit in the class and listen to the lecture. You have to ____________________ and pay for the course.

b. I went to ____________________ for the study group which the other students have organized.

4. | complicated   difficult |

"Why are there so many poor people in such a rich country?"

"The reasons are ____________________ . That's why it's ____________________ to explain."

5. | simple   easy |

____________________ explanations make things ____________________ .

8 Which of the words in exercise 6B would you use when talking about your past? Which would you use when talking about your present and which when talking about your future? Write them in the appropriate column on page 102. Then explain your choices to another student.

Example: I wrote *fail* under **My Past** because I failed a test when I was in high school. I wrote *require* under **My Future** because I hope that one day in the future I will not be required to do anything.

My Past	My Present	My Future

EXPANSION

FOCUS ON COLLOCATIONS: Some words are used together frequently. For example, we say ***take** a course*. We do not say ***do** a course*.

9 **A.** Which words in *italics* are used with the words in the boxes? Write the words in the blanks. (Note: You will need to use one word twice.)

academic *class* *course* *educational* *homework* *scholarship*

A

sign up for
take
drop
pass
fail

a ________
OR
a ________

B

cut
go to
attend
____

C

an ________ movie
program on TV

D

full
partial
academic
athletic
____

E

an ________ program at school
record
schedule
scholarship

F

do
mark
assign
____

B. Answer these questions with the words in parentheses and another word from the boxes in exercise 9A.

Example: (scholarship) What do students who play basketball on university teams often get? athletic scholarships

1. (homework) What do teachers do? ______
2. (academic) What is important to have in college? A good ______
3. (class) What do bad students do? ______
4. (scholarship) The college you want to go to costs $18,000. You have $10,000. You want the university to give you $8,000. What do you want?

   ______
5. (scholarship) What do universities often give good students who need money? ______

> **FOCUS ON GRADABLE ANTONYMS:** It is helpful to learn words that are opposite in meaning to each other, for example *bad* and *good*. It is also helpful to learn the words for degrees in between. For example, in between *bad* and *good* are the words *fair* and *okay*.

10 Below are six words often used to describe students. Write them in the right place on the line. (Note: Two words are similar in meaning. Put them together on the line.)

average bright brilliant slow smart dumb

brilliant

← **bad** | **good** →

> **FOCUS ON TOPIC-RELATED WORDS:** It is helpful to learn words related to the same topic.

11 **A.** Study the chart on page 104. It shows the typical system at an American college. Use your dictionary or check with another student to learn the meaning of any new words.

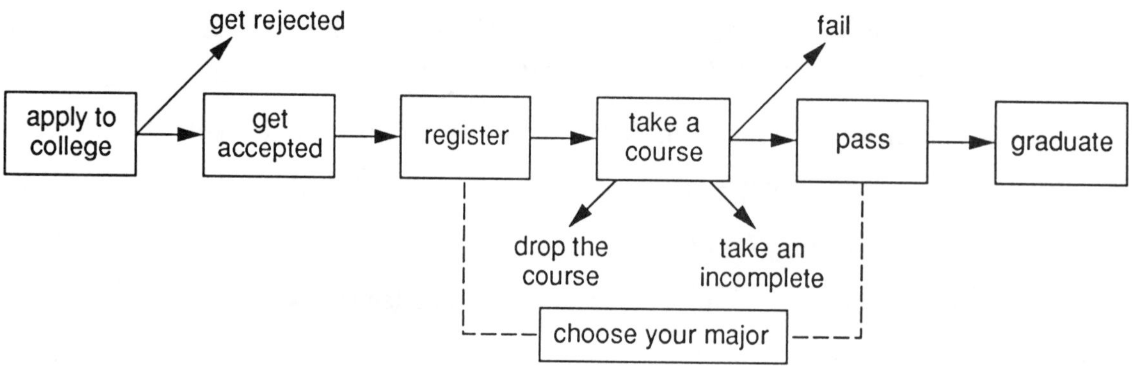

B. Compare the similarities and differences between the university systems in your country and the United States. Check (✔) any statements which are true about the university system in your country. Write *USA* next to any statements which are true about American colleges. Some statements may be true about your country and the USA. What are the good points and bad points of each system?

1. If you fail a course, you can take the course again and again until you pass it. ______
2. If you fail one or two courses during the year, you must repeat the whole year. ______
3. Generally, you must be a high school graduate to enter college. ______
4. People usually graduate from college after four years. ______
5. Students often decide what they are going to major in at the end of their second year of college. ______
6. Only graduates from certain high schools can go on to college. ______
7. If you can't complete the requirements of a course on time, you can take an incomplete and finish it later. ______
8. You must take electives, courses outside your major. ______
9. In order to pass a course, you must attend class. ______
10. The university helps students find jobs when they graduate. ______
11. Students don't have to pay to attend the university. ______
12. Students often meet with professors outside of class to ask questions or discuss problems. ______
13. Students often live on campus in buildings owned by the university. ______
14. Professors expect students to ask questions and express their opinions in class. ______

12 Play the game called Half a Minute. In groups of four to six students, cut up twelve pieces of paper and write down the following:

- the good points of dropping a course
- why learning English is easy
- the good points of having a hard teacher
- the good points of doing homework
- the bad points of having to attend class
- the bad points of majoring in math
- the good points of learning English
- the bad points of getting a degree
- the bad points of living on campus
- the good points of failing a test
- the bad points of being brilliant
- something that doesn't make sense

Fold the pieces of paper so that you cannot see what is written on them. Then the first player should pick one piece and talk for thirty seconds about the topic that is written on it. You get a point if, during this thirty-second period, you do not stop talking and you do not repeat yourself. When the first player is finished, it is the next player's turn. The game is over when all the topics have been discussed.

WORD STUDY

> **FOCUS ON COLLOCATIONS:** *Take* and *get* are sometimes similar in meaning, but they are used in different expressions. We say ***take** a course* but ***get** a good grade.*

13 **A.** Look at the words below. Write them under the correct verb.

a bad grade	a scholarship	a break
a course	a test	523 on the TOEFL
a high school diploma	a university degree	a certificate

Get	Take
get a bad grade	take a course

B. Ask another student these questions.

1. How old were you when you got your high school diploma?
2. When are you going to take a break?
3. Do you usually get good grades or bad grades?
4. When are you going to take your next test?
5. If you have ever gotten a scholarship, how much was it for?
6. Why did you decide to take an English course?
7. Will you get a certificate at the end of your English course?

FOCUS ON ADJECTIVES WITH PRESENT PARTICIPLE AND PAST PARTICIPLE ENDINGS: Adjectives ending in *-ing* have a different meaning from adjectives ending in *-ed*.

Study these examples: **a.** I was very *confused* during Professor Murnaghan's lecture.
b. Professor Murnaghan's lecture was very *confusing*.

The *-ed* ending shows how you felt (I felt *confus**ed***). The *-ing* ending shows how something or someone made you feel (The lecture made me feel *confus**ed***, so the lecture was *confus**ing***).

14 Complete the sentences with the words below. (Note: Do not use any word more than once.)

bored	confused	interested	shocked	tired
boring	confusing	interesting	shocking	tiring

1. I often get ____________ when I have to do the same thing again and again.
2. A good lecture is usually ____________________ .
3. A five-hour examination can be ____________________ .
4. I often feel ____________________ when I come home after a long day.
5. I often get ____________________ when I try to understand grammar rules.
6. I was ____________________ when I saw I had failed the exam. I thought I had done well.
7. What the teacher said was ____________________ . The explanation didn't help at all, and I still don't understand.
8. Students don't like it, but in school they have to do many ____________ things.
9. Are you ____________________ in studying at an American university?
10. The news was ________________ . I couldn't believe it when I heard it.

UNIT 9

THE WORKING WORLD

Do you know these words?

to hire	a position	an employer	economic
to fire	a firm	a manager	
to lay off	an industry	staff	

PRESENTATION

1 What is important to you in choosing a job? Put the factors below in order from the most important for you (write *1*) to the least important (write *10*). (Add anything else that is important to you.) Then explain your answers to another student.

a. The pay is good. ______

b. The work is interesting. ______

c. The work is helpful to society. ______

d. The hours are not long. ______

e. The boss is nice. ______

f. The people I work with are friendly. ______

g. There are opportunities for a better job in the future. ______

h. The job is near my home. ______

i. Nobody tells me what to do. ______

j. The hours are flexible: I work eight hours a day, but I decide the times of the day I work. ______

Other reasons ____

____

2 You are going to read an article about differences between working for Japanese companies and working for American companies. Before you read it, look at the words below. Check (✔) the words you think will definitely be in the text. Put an *X* next to the words you are certain will not be in the text. Put a question mark (?) next to the words you think may be in the text.

1. bosses ______
2. company ______
3. educated ______
4. hours ______
5. interview ______
6. jobs ______
7. lazy ______
8. salary ______
9. skills ______
10. vacation ______
11. bonuses ______

Read the article, and see if you were right.

Listen as you read the article.

Do It My Way

Misunderstandings between Japanese and American businessmen are possible any time. In fact, they can begin at the first interview. A big American company typically *hires* people to fill particular *positions.* Its bosses know that Americans easily change jobs and move to different parts of the country. As a result, jobs and the skills needed to fill them are clearly defined. American *firms hire* and *fire* whenever they want. In many *industries,* employees are often *laid off* in bad times and *rehired* when business improves.

The employment practices of Japanese companies could not be more different. They *hire* people more for the skills they will acquire after joining the company. Job descriptions identify only the minimum which the *firm* expects from its employees. Japanese *employers* want the people they *hire* to make a long-term commitment and to look constantly for ways to serve their company better.

Mazda and Chrysler, the Japanese and American car companies, responded completely differently to similar *economic* problems in the 1980s. Instead of cutting jobs, Mazda's *managers* agreed to a 25 percent salary cut and a loss of bonuses for four years. Chrysler, in contrast, cut its blue-collar[1] workforce by 28 percent, its white-collar[2] *staff* by 7 percent and its managers' pay by 2 to 10 percent.

[1]blue-collar: relating to workers who do hard or dirty work with their hands
[2]white-collar: relating to office workers

3 **A.** Write *Japanese* if the situation is typical, according to the information in the text, of a Japanese working situation. Write *American* if it is typical of an American working situation.

1. A worker works for a company for two years and then goes to work for another company. ____________
2. A worker works for the same company for most of his or her working life. ____________
3. What a worker does for a company changes quite a lot as time passes. ____________
4. What a worker does for a company changes very little as time passes. ____________
5. Businesspeople think it is bad for their companies if workers are changed often. ____________
6. If a company's business is bad, its workers will not be surprised to lose their jobs. ____________

B. Check (✔) the statements which are true about working situations in your country.

1. Workers work for the same company for most of their working lives. ______
2. People easily change jobs and move to different parts of the country. ______
3. If a company's business is bad, its workers will not be surprised to lose their jobs. ______
4. There are laws to protect workers from losing their jobs. ______
5. Businesspeople think it is bad for their companies if workers are changed often. ______

> **FOCUS ON GUESSING MEANING:** You can often guess the meaning (or general meaning) of a word if you look for clues which come before and/or after it.

4 **A.** Read the sentences and try to guess the meaning of the words in *italics*. When you think you know the meanings, go on to exercise 4B.

1. Guess what? I got the job with Database. The director just called to tell me I've been *hired*. I start next Monday.
2. Hello. I'm calling about the secretarial *position* that was advertised in this Sunday's paper. Could you tell me a little about the job?

3. The *firm* makes equipment for hospitals. The company also does research in new medical technology.
4. **A:** Why are you home from work so early?
   B: You're not going to believe this, but the boss *fired* me. She said the other workers had complained I was unfriendly and she didn't think I was the right person for the job.
5. The largest *industries* around here are the car *industry* and the clothing *industry*. More than 30 percent of the people in the area work in these factories.
6. *Employers* pay their workers and expect them to do a good job for the money they receive. They do not give jobs to people they think are lazy.
7. Hello, Sam. Won't you please come in and have a seat? First of all, I want you to know that we're very happy with your work here. However, I have some bad news. As you know, the company is having some problems, and we're going to have to *lay off* some people. I'm afraid you are one of them.
8. The *economic* situation is not good. Several companies in the area have closed down and other businesses are in trouble. For these reasons, it is difficult for people to find work.
9. I asked one of the people who works at the bank, but he was not very helpful. In fact, he was very rude, so I went to see the *manager*. She solved my problem quickly, said she was sorry for the way one of her workers had spoken to me and would make sure it didn't happen again.
10. We're having a party for all of the *staff* right before Christmas. We hope everyone who works here will attend.

B. Fill in each blank with the word below which is similar in meaning to the phrase on the right.

economic	fire	hire	lay off	position
employer	firm	industry	manager	staff

1. ____________________ ; ____________________ : boss
2. ____________________ : workers
3. ____________________ ; ____________________ : end a person's job
4. ____________________ : company
5. ____________________ : job
6. ____________________ : give a job to
7. ____________________ : related to business and/or money
8. ____________________ : type of work that usually gives jobs to many people, who use machinery to make things

C. Write down the parts of each sentence in exercise 4A which helped you guess the meaning of the word in *italics*.

1. hire: ____________________
2. position: ____________________
3. firm: ____________________
4. fire: ____________________
5. industry: ____________________
6. employer: ____________________
7. lay off: ____________________
8. economic: ____________________
9. manager: ____________________
10. staff: ____________________

5 List the words from the box which would be used in each situation. (You may need to use the words in the box more than once.) When you have finished, show your list to another student and explain how the words and situations are connected.

economic	an industry
an employer	to lay off
to fire	a manager
a firm	a position
to hire	staff

1. a job interview: ____________________
2. a newspaper article: ____________________
3. a job advertisement in a newspaper: ____________________
4. a conversation at work during lunch: ____________________
5. a business meeting: ____________________

EXPANSION

FOCUS ON TOPIC-RELATED WORDS: It is helpful to learn words that are related to the same topic.

6 **A.** Read the following statements. Use a dictionary to look up any new words. Then write the words and phrases in *italics* in the correct column.

1. "You've been late one too many times. *You're fired.*"
2. "If you're interested in the job, we'd like to *hire* you."
3. "I have good news. I think I'm going to *get a job* that pays $15 an hour."
4. "*I got a promotion*. Let's go out and celebrate."
5. "Business is bad, and the company is going to *lay off* fifty workers."
6. "It's clear that we workers are not going to get what we want. We have no choice but to *go on strike* and close the company down."
7. "They told me at work today that I'm going to *get a raise*. I hope it will be enough for us to buy a new car."
8. "I'm going to *retire* next year after thirty-five years with the company."
9. "I'm afraid I might *lose my job*. Business has been bad the past six months."
10. "My boss is becoming impossible. If things don't change, I'm going to *quit*."

At the beginning (when you first get a job)	**In the middle** (after you've had a job for a while)	**At the end** (just before you stop working at the job)

B. Use the words in *italics* in exercise 6A to make up a story about the work situations of two people, Person X and Person Y, over a period of time. Work with your partner and decide which words describe what happened to Person X and which words describe what happened to Person Y. Then write what happened to each person. Add any information you need to make your story complete. When you have finished, compare stories with another pair.

> **FOCUS ON SYNONYMS:** Some words may be similar. However, this does not mean that they have the exact same meaning or that they can be used in the exact same way.

7 **A.** In each box on page 114 are words which are similar in meaning but not identical. Look at the dictionary definitions. How are the words in each box different in meaning?

job occupation work profession position career

USAGE What you do to earn your living is your **job,** your **work,** or (more formal) your **occupation**: *Do you like your* **job?**|*Please state your name, age, and* **occupation** *on the form.* **Post** and **position** are more formal (words for a particular job): *Please send me details of the* **post/position** *which is advertised in today's paper.* A skilled job in which you use your hands is a **trade:** *She's an electrician by* **trade.** And a job for which you need special training and a high level of education (such as being a doctor or lawyer) is a **profession**. Some professions, such as teaching, nursing, and the Church, are also called **vocations**, which suggests that people do them in order to help others. A **career** is a job or profession that you follow for your whole life. *Her political* **career** *began when she was elected to the Senate 20 years ago.*

staff employee worker laborer

em·ploy·ee /ɪm'plɔɪ-iʸ, ˌɛmplɔɪ'iʸ, ɪm-/ *n* [*of*] a person who is employed: *a government employee*

la·bor·er *AmE*||**labourer** *BrE* /'leʸbəˌrər/ *n* a worker whose job needs strength rather than skill

staff[1] /stæf/ *n* the group of workers who do the work of an organization: *The school's teaching staff is excellent.*|*a staff of 15*|*She's* **on the staff of** *the new university*.

work·er /'wɜrkər/ *n* **1** a person or animal that works **2** a hard worker: *She's a real worker; she gets twice as much done as anybody else.* **3** also **workingman** /'wɜrkɪŋˌmæn/ a person who works with his hands, WORKING CLASS person: *a factory worker*

pay salary wages income

USAGE **Pay** is a general word for the money you receive from work, but **income** means any money you receive, whether from work or from money INVESTed, rents, etc.: *Have you any* **income** *apart from your pay?* **Remuneration** is like **pay**, but much more formal. **Wages** and **salary** are both **pay** received at regular times, but a **salary** is usually paid monthly or every two weeks, and **wages** are usually paid weekly and are calculated by the hour, day, or week. Money paid for certain professional services (e.g. to a lawyer) is a **fee.**

dismiss fire lay off

dis·miss /dɪs'mɪs/ *v* [T] **1** [*from*] *fml* to take away (the job of): *If you're late again you'll be dismissed (from you job).*

fire[2] *v* **fired, firing** [T] *infml*||also **sack** *BrE*– to dismiss from a job; *Get out! You're fired!*

lay sbdy.↔ **off** *v adv* [T] to stop employing (a worker), esp. for a period in which there is little work: *They laid us off for three months.*

B. Write one or two sentences about the differences in meaning between the pairs of words.

Example: *fire* and *dismiss* *Fire* is an informal word; *dismiss* is formal.

1. *job* and *occupation* ______________________
2. *work* and *profession* ______________________
3. *occupation* and *career* ______________________
4. *staff* and *employee* ______________________
5. *employee* and *worker* ______________________
6. *wages* and *salary* ______________________
7. *salary* and *income* ______________________
8. *fire* and *lay off* ______________________

> **FOCUS ON DERIVED FORMS:** When you learn a new word, it is useful to learn the other forms related to that word: the derived words.

8 **A.** Below are suffixes that can be used with the stem *econom* to form new words. Write the correct suffix in each blank. Use a dictionary if you need help.

-y *-ic* *-ical* *-ics* *-ize* *-ist*

1. Students in college often take courses in this: econom<u>ics</u>______ .
2. What makes a company close down: econom______ problems.
3. People buy small cars because they are this: econom______ .
4. Someone the President may talk to for an opinion on money matters: an econom______ .
5. What many newspapers write about: the econom______ .
6. What people do in order to save money: econom______ .

B. Below are suffixes that can be used with the stem *employ* to form new words. Write the correct suffix in each blank. (You will need to use two of the suffixes twice.)

-er *-ee* *-ment* *-ed*

1. A person with no job: unemploy______ .
2. A serious problem: unemploy______ .
3. 150 at a company: employ______ .
4. Someone who has a job: employ______ .
5. The kind of agency which helps people find jobs: employ______ .
6. The person who decides who to hire and fire: employ______ .

9 Play the Connection Game in groups of four to six students.

- **a.** The first player chooses two words from the chart and says how they are connected.
- **b.** The other players decide if this explanation is acceptable. If they accept the connection, the first player gets a point. Then these two words are crossed out; they cannot be used again.
- **c.** If the other players do not accept the first player's explanation, it is the next player's turn and the two words can still be used.
- **d.** The game is over when all the words have been used or when no one can think of any connections between the remaining words.

Examples: *lay off* and *fire* — They have a similar meaning.
unemployed and *salary* — If you are unemployed, you don't get a salary.

manager	firm (*n*)	lay off	employer
promotion	retire	industry	raise (*n*)
economical	employee	unemployed	economic
quit	hire	staff (*n*)	dismiss
unemployment	career	income	position
fire (*v*)	employ	interview (*n*)	company
salary	job	business	strike (*n*)
vacation	economy	colleague	skill

WORD STUDY

> **FOCUS ON THE GRAMMAR OF WORDS:** Some nouns can be countable or uncountable depending on their meaning. Countable nouns can be singular or plural. Uncountable nouns are neither singular nor plural, but they are used with a singular verb. A dictionary will tell you when a noun is countable or uncountable.

10 **A.** Study the dictionary entries for *business, company,* and *experience.* Notice when these words are countable and when they are uncountable.

busi·ness *n* **1** [C;U] one's work or employment: *I'm in the insurance business,|I'm here on business, not for pleasure.* **2** [U] trade and the getting of money: *"How's business?"* **3** [C] a particular money-earning activity or place, such as a shop: *to sell one's/the business*

com·pa·ny *n* **1** [C] a group of people combined together for business, trade, artistic purposes, etc: *a bus company|Which company do you work for?* **2** [U] companionship; fellowship: *I was glad I had Joan's company when I went to Boston.* **3** [U] companions; the people with whom a person spends time: *Sam's not been very good company these days.* **4** [U] one or more guests: *You can't go out tonight; we're expecting company.*

ex·pe·ri·ence *n* **1** [U] (the gaining of) knowledge or skill from practice rather than from books: *a teacher with five years' experience.* **2** [C] something that happens to one and has an effect on the mind and feelings: *Living through an earthquake was quite an experience.*

B. Read each sentence and find the correct definition of the word as it is used in the sentence. See if the word is countable [C] or uncountable [U] when it has this meaning. Complete the sentences with *a* or *an,* when necessary. Put a dash (—) if an article isn't needed.

1. They want to open ______ business in the downtown area.
2. ______ business is good.
3. I had ______ company for dinner at my place last night.
4. It's ______ company that makes shoes.
5. What I need is ______ company. I hate being alone all the time.
6. We are looking for people with ______ experience. You have not done this sort of work before.
7. I had ______ very strange experience on my way to work the other day.

FOCUS ON PREFIXES: A prefix is a group of letters added to the beginning of a word. You can change the meaning of a word by adding a prefix to it. The prefix *re-*, which often means "to do something again," can be used with certain verbs. For example, *rehire* means "to hire someone again."

11 **A.** You can use the prefix *re-* with eight of the following verbs. Write new verbs with *re-*. Cross out the two verbs which cannot be used with the prefix *re-*.

1. hire: rehire
2. schedule: ______
3. go: ______
4. write: ______
5. do: ______
6. tell: ______
7. read: ______
8. build: ______
9. look: ______
10. type: ______

B. Which of the eight verbs that take the prefix *re-* in exercise 11A can be used with the nouns below? (Note: There may be more than one correct answer, but be sure to use each verb at least once.)

1. a worker: ______
2. a composition: ______
3. a plan: ______
4. a story: ______
5. a bridge: ______
6. the directions: ______
7. an appointment: ______
8. a letter: ______

C. Not all words beginning with *re-* have the meaning of "do something again." Put an *X* next to the following words if *re-* does not mean "again."

1. remember______
2. rehire______
3. retire______
4. repay______
5. return ______
6. reapply______

REVIEW 3

1 Some words have a positive meaning. For example, if you graduate from college, you have completed your studies successfully. Therefore, *graduate* has a positive meaning. Other words have a negative meaning. For example, a student who is slow finds it difficult to do well in school. Therefore, *slow* has a negative meaning. Finally, some words have a neutral meaning. They have neither a positive nor a negative meaning.

Do the following words have a positive, a negative, or a neutral meaning? Check (✔) the appropriate column. When you have finished, compare answers with another student. You may disagree, so be sure to give the reasons for your answers.

	Positive	Negative	Neutral
1. attend	_______	_______	_______
2. brilliant	_______	_______	_______
3. dumb	_______	_______	_______
4. election	_______	_______	_______
5. eligible	_______	_______	_______
6. fail	_______	_______	_______
7. fire	_______	_______	_______
8. get a raise	_______	_______	_______
9. hire	_______	_______	_______
10. industry	_______	_______	_______
11. issue	_______	_______	_______
12. lay off	_______	_______	_______
13. make sense	_______	_______	_______
14. marcher	_______	_______	_______
15. partial scholarship	_______	_______	_______
16. protest	_______	_______	_______
17. quit	_______	_______	_______
18. retire	_______	_______	_______

2 How well do you know the derived forms of the words you studied in Units 7, 8, and 9? Read each dialogue. Complete the sentences with the correct form of the words in *italics*.

1. *economic*

   A: Why don't you shop at Burgess's Grocery Store anymore?

   B: Because it's more ________________ to shop at the supermarket. Prices are lower there.

2. *economic*

   A: Aren't you taking a vacation this year?

   B: No, we have to ________________ . My wife lost her job.

3. *employer*

   A: Are you ________________ ?

   B: Yes, I work for ANT. I'm a computer operator there.

4. *employer*

   A: I'm looking for ________________ in the car industry.

   B: It will be difficult. I hear they're not hiring.

5. *demonstration*

   A: Did you see all the ________________ as they walked by?

   B: Yes, there sure were a lot.

6. *oppose*

   A: The government has just announced that taxes are going to go up.

   B: You can be sure there will be a lot of ________________ to that.

7. *oppose*

   A: What happened to the President's ________________ in the last election?

   B: He became a professor at a university in Iowa.

8. *qualified*

   A: Can you explain to me why you won't hire me?

   B: Because you don't have the right ________________ .

9. *vote*

   A: Has the ________________ been counted?

   B: No, they still don't know who won the election.

10. *protest*

    A: There are a lot of police on the street.

    B: I guess they want to make sure nothing happens to the ________________ .

3 Look at the words in the box below. If a friend asked you what they mean, how would you teach them to your friend? Would you show a picture? Would you give an example? Would you demonstrate the meaning? Would you give a definition?

Write each word from the box in the appropriate column. When you have finished, compare lists with other students.

Example: A picture: *marcher*—
An example: *profession*—a doctor, a lawyer, a teacher
A demonstration: *assign*—ask your teacher what she or he is going to assign for homework tonight
A definition: *attend*—be present at

environmentalism	complicated	to dismiss
a party	to get rejected	a firm
a right	to graduate	to go on strike
terrorism	a major	staff

Show a Picture	Give an Example	Demonstrate the Meaning	Give a Definition

4 Read each dialogue. Rewrite the words in *italics* with one of the following prefixes: *dis-, in-, non-, re-, un-*.

Example: A: My papers show that I'm *qualified* to teach swimming.
B: No, I'm sorry. This paper shows that you're unqualified.

1. **A:** I thought you've been *employed* for the past six months.
   B: No, I've been ____________, and I have no hope of finding a job soon.
2. **A:** You said you *agree*.
   B: No, I said I ____________.
3. **A:** I'm very *experienced* in this kind of work.
   B: I'm afraid your co-workers say that you are very ____________.
4. **A:** I'm *eligible* to vote. I'm 18 years old.
   B: I'm sorry, but you're ____________. The voting age here is 21.
5. **A:** Why did you *type* this only once? I asked you to type it again.
   B: But I did ____________ it.
6. **A:** I *did* what you asked me to do. Is it okay?
   B: No, I'm afraid not. You'll have to ____________ it.
7. **A:** She's one of our most *honest* workers.
   B: I don't think you know her well. She's probably one of our most ____________ workers.
8. **A:** The advertisement said the special price was for *members*.
   B: No, it said it was for ____________.

5 Rewrite each sentence using the word in parentheses. Do not change the meaning.

1. They gave me the job. *(hire)*
   They hired me.
2. They aren't allowed to get married without their parents' permission. *(right)*
   ____
3. The teacher gave so much homework. *(assign)*
   ____

4. I've lost my job. *(lay off)*

____

5. You can apply for the scholarship. *(eligible)*

____

6. I don't understand anything. *(make sense)*

____

7. I didn't pass the test. *(fail)*

____

8. I go to every class. *(attend)*

____

9. The government has stopped allowing cars in the downtown area. *(ban)*

____

6 Play the game on the following page in groups of four. Each player uses a different box of words. Player A uses the words in box A, Player B uses the words in box B, Player C uses the words in box C, and Player D uses the words in box D. The number next to each word in the boxes is the point value of that word. Player A begins by writing down one of the words from his or her box next to *study* in the middle of the board. Then Player A must explain the connection between *study* and the word he or she has written down.

Example: *register/study* To study at a university, you must register for courses.

If the other players think that Player A's explanation is logical, he or she gets the points for using that word. (For example, if Player A uses *register* with *study,* he or she gets three points.) Then Player B writes down one of the words from his or her box next to *study* or next to the word Player A wrote down and explains the connection. (For example, if Player B uses *get accepted* with *register,* he or she gets five points, but if Player B uses *get accepted* with *study,* he or she gets only two points because *study* has no point value.) Player C can write down his or her word next to any of the words already on the board and explain the connection. The game is over when players cannot use any of the remaining words in their boxes. The player with the most points is the winner.

A	
ban	4
qualified	3
academic	3
average	2
register	3
career	1
manager	1
salary	2

B	
campaign	4
majority	3
racism	3
bright	2
get accepted	2
require	1
promotion	3
occupation	1

C	
candidate	3
oppose	4
apply	1
full scholarship	1
mark	3
sign up	3
income	2
employee	2

D	
demonstration	3
assign	3
confused	1
cut class	4
slow student	2
lose one's job	1
position	3
wages	2

				STUDY				

7 Listen to the story.

Now listen to the story again. On a piece of paper, write down what the speaker says.

8 **A.** You have learned many words in the past three units. They are listed below.

Unit 7	Unit 8	Unit 9
ban	academic	career
campaign	accept (get accepted)	dismiss
candidate	apply	economic
capitalism	assign	employee
communism	attend	employer
demonstration	average	fire (*v*)
election	bright	firm (*n*)
eligible	brilliant	hire
environmentalism	complicated	income
feminism	confused	industry
issue	cut class	lay off
majority	drop	lose one's job
marcher	dumb	manager
nationalism	fail	occupation
oppose	full scholarship	pay (*n*)
party	graduate (*v*)	position
protest	major (*n*)	profession
qualified	make sense	promotion (get a promotion)
racism	mark (*v*)	quit
right (*n*)	partial scholarship	raise (get a raise)
sexism	register (*v*)	retire
terrorism	reject (get rejected)	salary
	require	staff
	sign up	strike (go on strike)
	simple	wages
	slow	

B. It is difficult to remember and to use all of these words equally well. For example, some of the words you may be using already. Some of the words you may know the meaning of but are not comfortable using. Other words you may not remember at all. To help you check how well you know these words, write each of them in one of the following columns on page 126.

I Can Use These Words Correctly	I Know the Meaning of These Words, But I Can't Use Them Yet	I Think I Know the Meaning of These Words, But I'm Not Sure	I Don't Know These Words

C. You have probably found when learning new vocabulary that you do not always remember the same words after you have studied them. Words you think you know one week you can't remember at all the next week. Or this week you find yourself using words that last week you thought you didn't know. Look back at your columns of words on pages 43 and 85. Move any words you want to a different column. (From time to time, check your lists and move any words you want to a different column.)

UNIT 10

MONEY

Do you know these words?

value	well-off	broke	charge
possession	middle-class	wealthy	make a living
fee			can't afford

PRESENTATION

1 Do you agree or disagree with the following statements? Check (✔) *I agree, I partially agree,* or *I disagree.* Compare answers with other students. Give the reasons for your answers.

	I agree	I partially agree	I disagree
1. Money brings happiness.	______	______	______
2. Money is bad.	______	______	______
3. Rich people should give their money to poor people.	______	______	______
4. Having a lot of money can be a problem.	______	______	______
5. What someone does with money shows what kind of person he or she is.	______	______	______
6. People worry too much about money.	______	______	______
7. Getting money is the most important thing in many people's lives.	______	______	______

2 You are going to read an article in which a psychiatrist from California talks about the importance of money. Put a check (✔) next to any of the following subjects you think he will talk about. Put an *X* if you don't think he will talk about it. Put a question mark (?) if you're not sure.

1. How much money his clients—people who come to see the psychiatrist—pay him ______
2. How the psychiatrist spends his money ______
3. Why the psychiatrist's clients are not happy ______
4. If the psychiatrist thinks money is good or bad ______
5. Why money makes people unhappy ______

Read the article, and then check your answers.

Listen as you read the article.

Money Matters

Money isn't good or bad. It has no *value* in itself. What matters is what you do with it. There is more potential good than bad in money. But if people are going to spend their whole life chasing money, then it's bad. I see a lot of people who are like this.

Most of the people I see are rich. You have to be fairly *well-off* to come to see me. I *charge* $125 an hour, sometimes $140, depending on my mood. If I don't like you, I *charge* more. After all, I've got to *make a living* too. (Of course, if I see that someone who is poor or *middle-class* really wants my help, I never refuse to see him because he *can't afford* my normal *fee*. In fact, a few people who come to see me are *broke,* and I don't *charge* them anything.)

What I'm finding with my rich clients is that they are asking, "Is money what life's all about? I have a tennis court; I have a Jaguar. I have this and I have that." I tell them, "Yes, this is what life is all about. Life is breathing, laughing, fooling around, playing tennis." But they want more, and I don't know where to get it for them.

I think people want too much. If you've got your car, your family; if you're in good health, have a beautiful home; if you've got your tennis and sailing, your parties, your relaxing, what else do you want? This is all there is. I don't really see that there is more in this world.

These *wealthy* people are not happy with their *possessions*. They want to create a new world with their money. But they are not gods. All that their money is going to do is make them comfortable in the world we've got. But they aren't satisfied with that.

3 Read the statements on page 130 about the importance of money. Which person is most like you? Change any part of this person's statement so that it reflects your opinion. If none of the people's thoughts are like yours, write your own statement about the importance of money.

Person X

Money is very important to me. I worry a lot that I don't have enough now and I won't have enough in the future. I try to save as much as possible, and I feel bad after I buy something I don't really need.

Person Y

Money is not that important to me. I find that I don't need much money in order to live and I hardly ever worry about it. One should enjoy life, and I doubt that people who work all the time enjoy life very much.

Person Z

Money isn't everything, but it's important. I don't worry about it, but I like to spend it. I love getting new things. Every time I buy something, I find there's something else I would like to have. This is the way I enjoy myself.

> **FOCUS ON GUESSING MEANING:** You can often guess the meaning (or general meaning) of a word if you look for clues which come before and/or after it.

4 **A.** The words below appear in the article on page 129. Study how they are used in the article. Then read what two other psychiatrists have to say about money, and complete the sentences with the following words.

value	charge	middle-class	fee	wealthy
well-off	make a living	can't afford	broke	possessions

1. I try not to __________ (1) my clients too much. My usual __________ (2) is $45, but some pay $25 because they just __________ (3) to pay any more.

I have some clients who are __________ (4), but they still worry a lot about money. What I do is ask them to write down a list of their __________ (5), everything they own. Sometimes I also ask them to write down the __________ (6) of these things so that they have a dollar number in their heads. Then I ask them to burn the paper and imagine that everything on the paper is gone and that they are no longer __________ (7). They must be able to burn the paper and still feel good about themselves.

2. Rich people are not satisfied because they see that although they have everything they want, they still haven't found happiness. ________ (8) people are not satisfied because they only want to be rich. Poor people are the ones who have the real problem because they find it difficult just to ________ (9) and sometimes can't buy food because they're ________ (10) .

B. Check your understanding of the words in exercise 4A. Cross out the sentence which is NOT correct according to the meaning of the words in *italics*.

1. *broke*
a. Someone who is broke has no money.
b. Someone who is not poor can be broke, for example, when he or she has just finished shopping.
~~**c.** Only very poor people can be broke.~~

2. *can't afford*
If you can't afford to buy something,
a. it's expensive for you.
b. you don't have the money with you right now.
c. you would have money problems if you bought it.

3. *charge*
a. The person who charges you is selling you something.
b. If someone charges you $15, this is the amount you pay.
c. If you charge someone $15, you buy something for $15.

4. *fee*
a. Factory workers receive a fee.
b. Professional people such as doctors and lawyers receive a fee.
c. A fee is an amount of money someone pays you for your services.

5. *make a living*
When you make a living,
a. you make money from working.
b. you make enough money to buy what is necessary in life.
c. you become rich.

6. *middle-class*
A middle-class person
a. is not rich or poor.
b. is poor.
c. does not work with his or her hands; for example, he or she does not clean floors in a hospital.

7. *possessions*
Your possessions are things which
a. are yours.
b. someone has given you to use for a short period of time.
c. you have bought or people have given you as gifts.

8. *value*
   a. The value of a home is the price of the home.
   b. The value of a home is how much you could probably get for the home if you wanted to sell it.
   c. When you buy a home, you hope the value of the home will go up.

9. *wealthy*
   a. Someone who is wealthy is not rich or poor.
   b. Someone who is wealthy is rich.

10. *well-off*
   a. Someone who is well-off may be rich.
   b. If you are well-off, you don't have to worry, for example, about not having enough money for a nice home, for your children's education, and for your old age.
   c. Someone who is well-off is always rich.

5 In groups of four to six students, think of examples of how a poor person, a middle-class person, and a wealthy person would use the following words. Write your sentences in the blanks.

Example: A poor person: *I wish I weren't always broke.*
A middle-class person: *I always worry that one day I'll lose my job and be broke.*
A wealthy person: *I can't understand how people can be broke.*

1. *can afford*

   A poor person: ______________________________

   A middle-class person: ______________________________

   A wealthy person: ______________________________

2. *charge*

   A poor person: ______________________________

   A middle-class person: ______________________________

   A wealthy person: ______________________________

3. *a fee*

   A poor person: ______________________________

   A middle-class person: ______________________________

   A wealthy person: ______________________________

4. *make a living*

   A poor person: ______________________________

   A middle-class person: ______________________________

   A wealthy person: ______________________________

5. *possessions*

A poor person: ______

A middle-class person: ______

A wealthy person: ______

6. *value*

A poor person: ______

A middle-class person: ______

A wealthy person: ______

7. *well-off*

A poor person: ______

A middle-class person: ______

A wealthy person: ______

EXPANSION

> **FOCUS ON TOPIC-RELATED WORDS:** It is helpful to learn words related to the same topic.

6 **A.** In the following box are twelve verbs connected to money. Some of the verbs are written from top to bottom, some from left to right, some from right to left, and some diagonally. With a partner, find the verbs, circle them, and write them in the correct column below.

Money Coming into Your Pocket	Money Going out of Your Pocket
	spend

W	B	L	W	A	S	T	E
I	N	H	E	R	I	T	A
T	S	E	V	N	I	Y	R
H	S	P	E	N	D	A	N
D	E	P	O	S	I	T	M
R	B	S	T	E	A	L	A
A	X	M	Q	Y	D	V	K
W	O	R	R	O	B	F	E

B. What other verbs can you add to the list in 6A? Do they describe money coming into or money going out of your pocket?

C. Which verbs in exercise 6A do you think go together? Do you think *borrow* and *lend* go together? Or do you think *borrow* and *waste* go together? Use the twelve verbs in 6A to make a list of six pairs of verbs which you think go together. Compare lists with another student. If there are any differences, explain your answer.

1. ______________ and ______________
2. ______________ and ______________
3. ______________ and ______________
4. ______________ and ______________
5. ______________ and ______________
6. ______________ and ______________

7

A. The following sentences are from two conversations. One conversation is between a husband and wife at a store. The other conversation is between a customer and a salesperson in the store. With your partner, separate the two conversations. Write the correct letters in the correct order in the blanks below.

a. I don't know. It's not as expensive as all the other sweaters we've seen, but do you think it's worth $50? It doesn't look well made.

b. No, there's no charge.

c. This is a gift for my mother. If she doesn't like it, can she return it?

d. As long as she has the receipt, she can exchange it. And if she can't find anything in the store she likes, we'll give her a full refund.

e. How about this sweater? The price is reasonable, and it looks like the kind of thing your mother would wear.

f. And is there a charge to have it gift wrapped?

1. What did the husband and wife say to each other? Write the letters.

____

2. What did the customer and salesperson say to each other? Write the letters.

____

B. Underline all the words in the conversations in exercise 7A which are connected to money.

C. Write *T* next to the facts which are true in your country.

1. The price of gas is reasonable. ______
2. When you buy something, the salesperson will not give you a receipt unless you ask for one. ______
3. If you return a gift to a store, you can always get a refund. ______
4. When you buy a TV, there is no charge for repairs. ______
5. Certain animals are worth a lot of money. ______

> **FOCUS ON GRADABLE ANTONYMS:** It is helpful to learn words that are opposite in meaning to each other, for example *bad* and *good.* It is also helpful to learn the words for degrees in between. For example, in between *bad* and *good* are the words *fair* and *okay.*

8 Write the words from each box in the right place on the line. (Note: Some words are similar in meaning. Put them together on the line.)

1.

cheap	expensive	high	inexpensive	moderately expensive	reasonable

____

← **less** ————————— **more** →

2.

comfortable	poor	wealthy	well-to-do	well-off

____

← **less** ————————— **more** →

3.

lower-class	lower middle-class	middle-class
upper-class	upper middle-class	working-class

____

← **less** ————————— **more** →

9 In English, we talk of people who go "from rags to riches." These people go from being very poor to being very rich. The following graph shows the rags-to-riches story of Jack Porter, from the time he was 20 years old and had no job, until his death at the age of 80, when he died a multimillionaire.

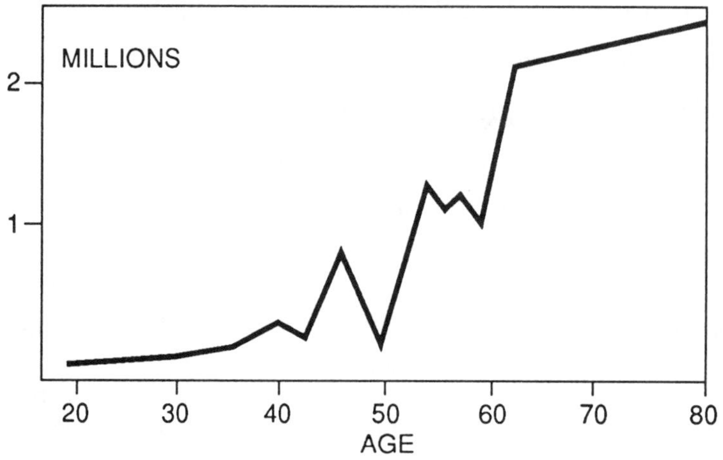

In groups of three to five students, discuss what you think happened to Jack in his lifetime. Then, using as many words as possible from the unit, write a story of how he went from rags to riches. Give as many details as possible. Say how he made money, how he lost money, and how his lifestyle changed over the years. When you have finished, exchange stories with the other groups. Which group correctly used the most words from this unit?

WORD STUDY

FOCUS ON THE GRAMMAR OF WORDS: Some adjectives can come before or after a noun. For example, we can say, "That woman is rich" or "She's a rich woman." However, some adjectives can only come after the noun. For example, we say, "Some people are afraid of money" (NOT: "They're afraid people").

10 Put an *X* next to the sentence if the adjective is not in the correct position. Then correct the sentence. Check your dictionary or ask your teacher if you are not sure.

Example: ______ Some people are *afraid.* ______________________

__X__ The afraid people are there. The people who are afraid are there.

______ 1. I can't go out to dinner. I'm *broke.* ______________________

____

______ 2. A *broke* friend of mine wants to borrow some money. ______________________

____

______ 3. *Wealthy* people live in that home. ______________________

____

______ 4. I wish we were *wealthy.* ______________________

____

______ 5. My brother is quite *well-off.* ______________________

____

______ 6. My *well-off* brother is going to lend me some money. ______________________

____

______ 7. People on the street who ask for money are often *poor.* ______________________

____

______ 8. Those children all come from *poor* families. ______________________

____

> **FOCUS ON SUFFIXES:** A suffix is a group of letters added to the end of a word. The suffix *-able* often means "able to be done." For example, if something is affordable, it can be afforded. However, the suffix *-able* does not always have this meaning. For example, something that is valuable is worth a lot of money.

11 **A.** Put a check (✔) in the blank if the *-able* ending of each word in *italics* means "able to be done."

1. "Come to M & B's for the most *affordable* prices in town!" ______
2. The paintings stolen from the museum were extremely *valuable.* ______
3. This is *payable* by check or money order. ______
4. These items are *returnable.* ______ You can exchange them for something else in the store.
5. However, your money is not *refundable.* ______
6. "The price is *reasonable.* Let's buy it." ______
7. "I don't need to be wealthy. I only want to be *comfortable.*" ______

B. On a separate piece of paper, make a list of the other adjectives you know which end in *-able.* Check (✔) the word if the ending means "able to be done." Compare lists with another student. Are there any more words to add to your list?

UNIT 11

HOME LIFE

Do you know these words?

charge	responsibility	share	devote	domestic
task	routine	raise	support	
care				

PRESENTATION

1 How are the lives of men and women in the present different from the lives of men and women in the past? How do you think the lives of men and women will be in the future? Write the following notes in the appropriate columns. Then compare answers with other students.

- Most women are housewives.
- Women are responsible for taking care of children.
- Husbands and wives both do housework.
- Husbands and wives are both responsible for making money for the family.
- Husbands make decisions about money.
- Fathers make decisions about their children's future.
- Wives do what husbands tell them to do.
- Most women work outside the home.
- Men and women do the same type of work outside the home.
- Men make more money than women make for the same job.

In the Past	Now	In the Future

2 The following words appear in this unit's reading. With another student, use the words to predict what the text is about.

1. In 1737 . . . more than 98 percent . . . women . . . England . . . worked outside the home
2. By 1911 . . . more than 90 percent . . . housewives
3. In the nineteenth century, factory and mine owners . . . hired whole families
4. . . . continued . . . two reasons . . . First . . . infants died . . . Moreover . . . terrible conditions in which these people lived . . . less and less able to do a good day's work
5. . . . machines . . . fewer workers . . . needed
6. . . . women . . . taking care . . . homes . . . Furthermore, only one wage . . . to the man of the house

Read the text, and then check your answers.

Listen as you read the article.

Domestic Chores Weren't Always Women's Work

In 1737, more than 98 percent of married women in England worked outside the home. By 1911, more than 90 percent were employed only as housewives. Did women in the industrialized world get together over tea one afternoon and agree to take *charge* of all the *domestic tasks* of cleaning, cooking, and child *care*? Did they decide they did not want to *share* any of the household *responsibilities*? No, they had little choice.

In fact, the housewife role is a very recent one. In the nineteenth century, factory and mine owners did not care who worked for them and hired whole families to make cloth and dig coal. It might have continued that way if it weren't for two reasons.

First, many infants died in the terrible conditions of working-class slums. Babies were left alone in dirty rooms, to free their mothers for work in the factories. Moreover, the terrible conditions in which these people lived and the tiring *routine* of their daily lives made them less and less able to do a good day's work.

Meanwhile, as machines became efficient, fewer workers were needed to operate them—which was the second reason women were removed from the workplace.

In the end, it was more profitable for a business to have women *devote* their time to taking care of their homes and *raising* their children. Furthermore, only one wage would need to be paid—to the man of the house—to *support* the family.

3 In each blank, write *Mostly men, Mostly women, Men and women,* or *Nobody.*

	1737	1911
1. worked in places like factories and mines	__________	__________
2. worked in the home	__________	__________
3. earned money outside the home	__________	__________
4. took care of babies	__________	__________
5. kept the house clean	__________	__________

> **FOCUS ON GUESSING MEANING:** You can often guess the meaning of a word (or general meaning) if you look for clues which come before and/or after it.

4 **A.** Try to guess the missing words in the following article.

Changing Times

Make room for Daddy. His role is changing. In the past, fathers were expected to __________ (1) the family, and it was also their job to make sure the children behaved.

But today, more and more fathers help with the kids and are involved in the daily __________ (2) of the household. They do all sorts of __________ (3) they had never done before. They take their children to the doctor, and instead of reading the newspaper in the evening, men are reading their children a book.

Although fathers are doing more, most still do less than their wives in __________ (4) duties—even when both parents work—and they know it. Almost three-quarters of the fathers in a recent study said they should be doing more to help __________ (5) the children, but only 13 percent __________ (6) child __________ (7) equally with their wives. What stops them from changing their ways?

Some have accepted their new roles only because they have had to; their wives also work, so they have little choice. Others feel unsure of themselves when taking care of children, especially because their wives usually __________ (8).

There is another reason. On the one hand, we say men should be __________ (9) fathers. On the other, we also think they should work long hours and be successful. The list of __________ (10) has gotten longer, and more and more fathers are asking what is going to come off of that list.

B. Here are the words missing from the article.

care	domestic	responsibilities	shared	take charge
devoted	raise	routine	support	tasks

These words all appeared in the article on page 140. Look again at how they were used there. Then complete the article in exercise 4A, and compare the answers with your first guess.

C. Write a definition, synonym, or translation for each word. (Note: If you write down a translation, check a bilingual dictionary to see if you guessed correctly.)

1. care: __________
2. devoted: __________
3. domestic: __________
4. raise: __________
5. responsibility: __________
6. routine: __________
7. share: __________
8. support: __________
9. charge: __________
10. task: __________

5 Do you agree or disagree with the following statements on page 143? Check (✔) *I agree, I partially agree,* or *I disagree.* Compare answers with other students. Give the reasons for your answers.

	I agree	I partially agree	I disagree
1. Taking care of the home and raising children are more difficult than working outside the home.	________	________	________
2. A woman's work is never done.	________	________	________
3. Women who work outside the home would prefer to be housewives.	________	________	________
4. Men should share in the household responsibilities.	________	________	________
5. Supporting the family is a man's responsibility.	________	________	________
6. It is impossible to be a good mother, wife, and working woman all at the same time.	________	________	________

6 Which of the following words do you associate with women? Which do you associate with men? Write the words in the appropriate columns. Then explain your answers to another student.

charge	task	share	routine	raise
domestic	care	responsibility	devote	support

Women	Men

EXPANSION

FOCUS ON COLLOCATIONS: *Responsibility* and *charge* are used in different expressions. We say ***take*** *charge* ***of*** and ***have*** *responsibility* ***for***.

7 **A.** There are seven phrases in this word snake. Can you find them? Circle the phrases and write them in the blanks that follow.

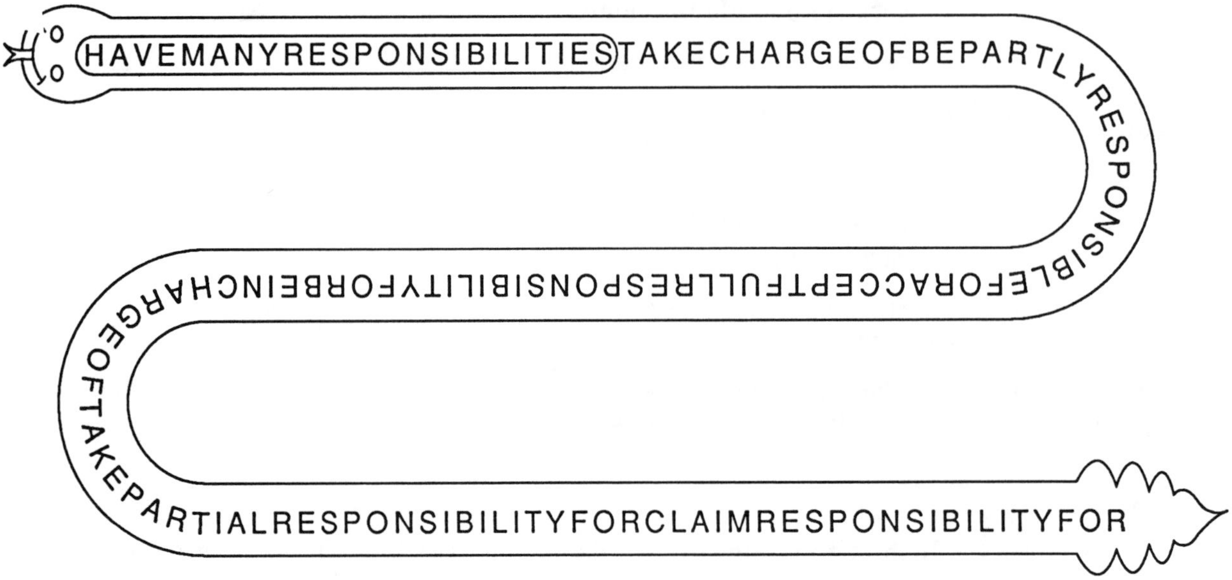

1. have many responsibilities
2. ____________________
3. ____________________
4. ____________________
5. ____________________
6. ____________________
7. ____________________

B. Use the information in exercise 7A to answer the following questions. Write the answers in the blanks.

1. Which verbs are used with *responsibility*? ____________________, ____________________, ____________________, and ____________________
2. Which adjectives are used with *responsibility*? ____________________ and ____________________
3. We say ***fully*** *responsible* and ***partially*** *responsible*. What other adverb is used with *responsible*? ____________________
4. What preposition is used with *responsibility* and *responsible*? ____________________

8 Read the following sentences. Explain who might be talking and give the reason for the person's comment.

Example: "I'm not responsible. Don't look at me."
Possible answer: It could be a boy telling his father he didn't break his father's favorite pipe.

1. "Who's in charge here?"
2. "You need to devote more time to your studies."
3. "She's been receiving very good care."
4. "I accept full responsibility for what happened."
5. "Please take charge while I'm gone."
6. "You need to make some changes in your daily routine."
7. "I don't have enough for everyone, so you'll have to share."
8. "I was raised to respect my elders. I would never do such a thing."

> **FOCUS ON SYNONYMS:** Some words may be similar. However, this does not mean that they have the exact same meaning or that they can be used in the exact same way.

9 **A.** Sometimes words similar in meaning are different in grammar. Study the following sentences. Then answer the questions.

I *grew up* in Hawaii.
I *was raised* in Hawaii.
I *was brought up* in Hawaii.

My grandmother *raised* me.
My grandmother *brought* me *up*.

1. Which verb often appears in passive form—*raise* or *grow up*?

 ____

2. Which verb always appears in active form—*raise* or *grow up*?

 ____

3. Which verb often appears in passive form—*bring up* or *grow up*?

 ____

4. Which verb always appears in active form—*bring up* or *grow up*?

 ____

5. Why is it wrong to say "I was grown up by my aunt"?

 ____

B. Sometimes words similar in meaning are different in the ideas which the words suggest. *Task, job,* and *chore* are all connected to a piece of work to be done. Study the following sentences. Then answer the questions.

This is a difficult *task*. It will take me at least a week to finish it.

I've got a *job* for you to do. It won't take long.

It is such a *chore* to do the shopping every day.

1. Which word means the work will probably be difficult—*task* or *chore*?

   ____

2. Which word means the work probably takes a short time—*task* or *chore*?

   ____

3. Which word means you probably do the work regularly—*job* or *chore*?

   ____

4. Is a chore interesting work? ____________________
5. What chores do you do every week? ____________________

C. Sometimes words similar in meaning go together with different words. *Domestic* and *household* both refer to "of the house and family," but as adjectives they often go together with different nouns. Study the words in the boxes below. Then answer the questions.

domestic: problems argument help violence chores responsibilities

household: expenses appliances pets chores responsibilities

1. Who might have a domestic argument? ____________________
2. What is an example of a household appliance? ____________________
3. What is an example of a household expense? ____________________
4. Newspapers often have ads for domestic help. What is another word for someone who does this sort of work? ____________________
5. There are often reports in the newspaper about domestic violence. What may have happened in such situations? ____________________

D. Sometimes words similar in meaning are different because one word is more formal than the other. Read the sentences. Then answer the questions.

1. a. Sweetheart, answer the phone. I'm trying to take care of the baby.
   b. He cared for his elderly aunt throughout her long illness.

Which is more formal—*take care of* or *care for*? ________________

2. a. Billy, care for your little sister until I get home from work, okay?
   b. Billy, take care of your little sister until I get home from work, okay?

Which sentence sounds better? ________________

> **FOCUS ON TOPIC-RELATED WORDS:** It is helpful to learn words related to the same topic.

10 **A.** Write down another way of saying the following expressions.

Example: do the ironing: iron the clothes

1. do the floor: ________________
2. do the laundry: ________________
3. do the shopping: ________________
4. do the dishes: ________________
5. do the windows: ________________
6. make dinner: ________________

B. How often do you do these tasks? Check (✔) *Every day, Almost every day, Sometimes, Hardly ever,* or *Never.*

	Every day	Almost every day	Some-times	Hardly ever	Never
make the bed	____	____	____	____	____
do the dishes	____	____	____	____	____
set the table	____	____	____	____	____
sweep the floor	____	____	____	____	____
mop the floor	____	____	____	____	____
dust	____	____	____	____	____
vacuum	____	____	____	____	____
iron	____	____	____	____	____
take out the trash	____	____	____	____	____
do the laundry	____	____	____	____	____
clean the bathroom	____	____	____	____	____

C. Look at the words below. Check with another student or use your dictionary to find the meaning of any new words. Which of these items would you use to do the tasks? Write the correct items in the blank next to each task. (Note: Some items may be used with more than one task.)

mop broom pillow dish sheet blanket iron water ironing board soap bucket vacuum cleaner dustpan silverware dustcloth trashcan washing machine dishwasher

1. make the bed: ____________________
2. do the dishes: ____________________
3. set the table: ____________________
4. sweep the floor: ____________________
5. mop the floor: ____________________
6. dust: ____________________
7. vacuum: ____________________
8. iron: ____________________
9. take out the trash: ____________________
10. do the laundry: ____________________
11. clean the bathroom: ____________________

11 Here are ten answers to questions from an interview. In groups of three, write an appropriate question for each answer. You must decide if the person answering the question is a man or a woman, and each question must contain a different word from this unit. When you have finished, exchange questions with another group.

- "Not really. But someone has to do it."
- "We both do, but I'm home more so I'm more involved."
- "It has its difficult moments, but all in all I enjoy it."
- "I imagine they do, but I can't say definitely."
- "It sometimes feels strange, but I'm used to it now."
- "I haven't really thought about that, I must admit."
- "Yes."
- "Ironing."
- "I agree."
- "Of course."

WORD STUDY

FOCUS ON HOMONYMS: One word in English can have more than one meaning. In this unit, the word *care* appears several times but with different meanings.

Housewives *take care of* their children.
Mine owners didn't *care* who did their work for them.

12 Study the meaning of the word in *italics* in each set of three sentences. In two of the sentences, the meaning of the word is the same. Cross out the sentence in which the meaning of the word is different.

Example: **a.** Mine owners didn't *care* who did their work for them.
~~**b.** Housewives take *care* of their children.~~
c. "Where do you want to have dinner?" "I don't *care*."

1. **a.** I can't *support* my family on the money I earn.
   b. I *support* all of your newest ideas.
   c. Parents often expect their children to *support* them in their old age.
2. **a.** If you want to ask something, *raise* your hand.
   b. I was *raised* in Philadelphia.
   c. His parents died when he was young, so his grandmother *raised* him.
3. **a.** I'm in *charge* of the music for the party.
   b. The mechanic *charged* me $300 to fix the car.
   c. Please take *charge* of the office while I'm gone.
4. **a.** I'm not very *domestic;* I hate cooking and cleaning.
   b. Peggy and Ed have had *domestic* troubles for years, but they're still married.
   c. When you arrive at the airport, go to Terminal A for *domestic* flights and Terminal B for international flights.

FOCUS ON THE PRONUNCIATION OF DERIVED FORMS: There is often a change in stress when, for example, an adjective is changed to a noun. The stress in the noun *responsibility* is on *-bil-,* the third syllable from the end. The stress in the adjective *responsible* is on *-spon-*.

13 **A.** All of the adjectives in column A on page 150 have appeared in previous units. In column B, write the nouns formed from these adjectives. Then underline the stressed syllable of the adjectives and nouns.

A	B
1. responsible	responsibility
2. able	
3. domestic	
4. fatal	
5. legal	
6. moral	
7. reliable	
8. simple	
9. stable	
10. stupid	

B. Look again at the stressed syllable of each noun in exercise 13A. Can you think of a rule for the position of the stress in nouns ending in *-ity*?

____

C. When there is a change in stress, there is often a change in vowel sounds. Use your dictionary to find the vowel sounds of the underlined letters in the adjective and noun forms. Write each vowel sound between the brackets (/   /).

1. able	/ /	ability	/ /
2. fatal	/ /	fatality	/ /
3. legal	/ /	legality	/ /
4. moral	/ /	morality	/ /
5. stable	/ /	stability	/ /

D. With other students practice saying the adjectives and nouns in exercise 13A. They should say which syllable you have stressed.

UNIT 12

CRIME AND PUNISHMENT

Do you know these words?

to accuse	to convict	to imprison	a trial	innocent
to charge	to fine	to sentence	an offense	
to commit				

PRESENTATION

1 **A.** All the words in column A are crimes. Match these words with their meaning in column B. Check with another student or use your dictionary to find the meaning of any words which are new.

A	B
1. arson	**a.** the crime of bringing things into one country from another without paying the necessary tax
2. burglary	**b.** the crime of entering a building and stealing
3. murder	**c.** the crime of selling the secrets of one country to another country
4. rape	**d.** the crime of setting fire to a building in order to destroy it
5. kidnapping	**e.** the crime of killing someone
6. shoplifting	**f.** the crime of forcing someone to have sex
7. smuggling	**g.** the crime of taking something from a store without paying
8. treason	**h.** the crime of taking someone in order to get money for his or her return

B. Now list the crimes in order of seriousness: List the most serious first and the least serious last. Compare answers with another student.

1. ____________________ **5.** ____________________

2. ____________________ **6.** ____________________

3. ____________________ **7.** ____________________

4. ____________________ **8.** ____________________

2 This unit's reading is an article about prisons. What do you know about prisons? Write *T* if you think the statement is true. Write *F* if you think the statement is false.

1. Prisons have existed for more than 500 years. ______

2. The prison system began as a way to help criminals. ______

3. At one time, people in prison in America had to pay for staying there. ______

Read the article, and then check your answers.

Listen as you read the article.

How Did Our Prisons Get That Way?

Prisons are a fact of life in America. We now keep a larger part of our population in prisons than any other nation except Russia and South Africa, and for longer periods of time. In fact, we Americans invented prisons. The first one was created in Philadelphia, Pennsylvania, in 1790, and the use of prisons soon spread from there to other cities in the United States and Europe.

While institutions like the Bastille in France and the Tower of London in England existed, they held mainly political prisoners, not ordinary criminals. Before there were prisons, people who *committed* serious crimes almost always received corporal or capital punishment; that is, they were punished either by being hurt physically or by death. Jails existed, but primarily for the *accused* while they awaited *trial.* The closest thing to the modern prison was the workhouse, a place of hard labor almost always for minor offenders. When a criminal was *convicted,* he was punished bodily or *fined* a certain amount of money but he was not *imprisoned.* Today's system, where imprisonment is a common punishment for a serious crime, is a modern one.

In the eighteenth century the greatest call for change in America came from the Quakers, a Christian group against violence who felt that prisoners were treated badly. They lived mostly in and around the nation's most important city, Philadelphia. At that time, Philadelphia jails locked up men and women in the same rooms at night. Prisoners were thrown together; their age, seriousness of *offense,* or ability to defend themselves was of no importance. And those *charged* with a crime had to pay for their own imprisonment even if they were found *innocent* at their *trial.*

In 1786 the Quakers persuaded the Pennsylvania lawmakers to *sentence* to death only those people *convicted* of the most serious crimes: murder, treason, rape, and arson. People *convicted* of less serious *offenses,* such as robbery or burglary, would have to give up their possessions and be *imprisoned* for ten years. Then in 1787, under pressure from the Quakers, the lawmakers agreed to change a Philadelphia jail into a prison for *convicted* criminals from across the state. It was designed for two kinds of prisoners: Serious offenders would be kept alone in sixteen jail cells; less serious ones would sleep in large rooms and work together in shops during the day. This became the first prison as we know it.

3 Check (✔) the sentences below that are correct according to the information in the text. Write *DS* if the text doesn't say.

1. In the 1700s a murderer in France could stay in the Bastille for a long time. ______
2. In the 1700s murderers were usually sent to a workhouse for a long time. ______
3. Before 1786 people in Pennsylvania who were convicted of robbery were sentenced to death. ______
4. The Quakers thought it was wrong to keep men and women accused of a crime in the same place. ______
5. The Quakers thought it was wrong to keep murderers in the same place with people who stole apples. ______
6. The first prison, which was started in Philadelphia, was a successful one. ______

4 Discuss these questions in groups.

1. Some countries, such as the United States, have serious crime problems, but other countries do not. What do you think is the reason for this difference?
2. In a number of states in the United States, a murderer can be sentenced to death (capital punishment). Is there capital punishment in your country? Do you believe in capital punishment? Or do you think murderers should remain in prison for their entire lives? Why?
3. In some countries the punishment for criminals is injury to their body (corporal punishment). Is there corporal punishment in your country? Do you believe in corporal punishment? Why? Why not?
4. Why do you think it is important to punish a person convicted of a crime? Is it to make the criminal suffer? Stop the criminal from committing other crimes? Prevent other people from committing the same kind of crime? Can you suggest other reasons?

FOCUS ON GUESSING MEANING: When you read, it is important to try to guess the meaning (or general meaning) of new words from the context.

5 **A.** The words below are from the reading on page 153. Read again the sentences in which the following words appear. Try to understand their meaning from the context. Then read the conversation below and write each word in the correct blank.

commit	trial	fine	offense	innocent
accused of	convicted of	imprisoned	charged with	sentence

[Jack is talking to his lawyer at the police station.]

Lawyer: You are ________ (1) robbery and your brother is ________ (2) shoplifting.

Jack: But we didn't ________ (3) any crime.

Lawyer: I don't know anything about that. All I know is that your ________ (4) begins on December 10.

Jack: And what will happen to us after that?

Lawyer: Well, if you're found ________ (5), you'll be free to go home. If you are ________ (6) robbery, the judge could ________ (7) you to up to fifteen years in prison.

Jack: But I didn't do anything!

Lawyer: I told you, I don't know anything about that.

Jack: And what about my brother?

Lawyer: The judge may ________ (8) him up to $5,000.

Jack: But he took a shirt that cost only $65!

Lawyer: Then, why didn't he pay for it? Shoplifting may not be a serious ________ (9), but it is still a crime. Anyway, don't worry about your brother. You're the one with the big problem. Don't you understand that you could be ________ (10) for fifteen years?

Jack: But I didn't do anything!

5 **B.** Check your understanding of the words in exercise 5A by completing the following statements.

1. When people are *imprisoned,* they go to ________________ .
2. When people are *fined,* they must ________________ .
3. Someone who is *innocent* has not done anything ________________ .

4. A person can be *convicted* of a robbery. A person cannot be convicted of coming home late. A person can only be *convicted* of a ________________ .
5. If a man kills another person, he has *committed* murder. If he kills himself, he has *committed* suicide. *Commit* means "do something that is ________________ ."
6. A judge can *sentence* someone, but a mother cannot *sentence* her child. *Sentence* someone means "give a punishment to someone after a ________________ ." Only a judge or court can do that.
7. Parking in a No-Parking area is an *offense*. It is not a *crime*. Robbery is an *offense*. It is also a *crime*. An *offense* can be serious or not serious. A *crime* is ________________ .
8. Anyone can *accuse* another person of stealing, but only the police can *charge* a person with stealing. You can *accuse* a friend of breaking your radio, but you can't *charge* him or her with breaking your radio.
   a. *Accuse* means that someone says another person has ________________ or has ________________ .
   b. *Charge* means that the police make a spoken or written statement which says a person has ________________ .

> **FOCUS ON COLLOCATIONS:** Some words are used together frequently. For example, we talk about a ***serious*** *crime* or a ***minor*** *offense.*

6 Which words in *italics* are used with the words in the boxes? Write the words in the blanks. (Note: Use each word only once.)

be *a crime* *stand* *suicide*
be on *murder* *find someone*

A	B	C
________ innocent ________	________ trial ________	to commit murder ________ ________

7 Put the following events in the order in which they usually occur.

a. You are charged. ______

b. You commit an offense. ______

c. You are convicted. ______

d. You are fined and/or imprisoned. ______

e. You are sentenced. ______

f. You stand trial. ______

EXPANSION

> **FOCUS ON DERIVED FORMS:** When you learn a new word, it is useful to learn the other forms related to that word: the derived words.

8 Write the derived forms of the words in *italics*. (Use a dictionary if you need help and be sure to check the pronunciation of the derived words.)

Noun	Noun (the Person)	Verb	Adjective
a crime	**1.** *a* criminal		
an offense	**2.** *an* __________		
punishment		**3.** *to* __________	
a trial		**4.** *to* __________	
5. *an* __________		*to accuse*	
6. *a* __________		*to charge*	
7. *a* __________	**8.** *a* __________	*to convict*	
9. *a* __________		*to fine*	
10. __________		*to imprison*	
11. *a* __________		*to sentence*	
12. __________			*innocent*

> **FOCUS ON TOPIC-RELATED WORDS:** It helps to remember words related to the same topic.

9 **A.** All the words below are related to crime. Check with another student or use your dictionary to find the meaning of any new words.

accuse	court	kidnapping	robbery
arrest	criminal	lawyer	sentence
arson	evidence	life imprisonment	steal
break into	fine	mugging	suspect
burglary	guilty	murderer	trial
capital punishment	innocent	police	victim
charge	judge	prisoner	weapon
convict	jury	rape	witness

B. Fill in the diagram with twenty of the words from exercise 9A. (You may add more circles to the diagram and/or more words to the list if you wish.) Put the words which are closely related near each other. When you have finished, compare diagrams with another student.

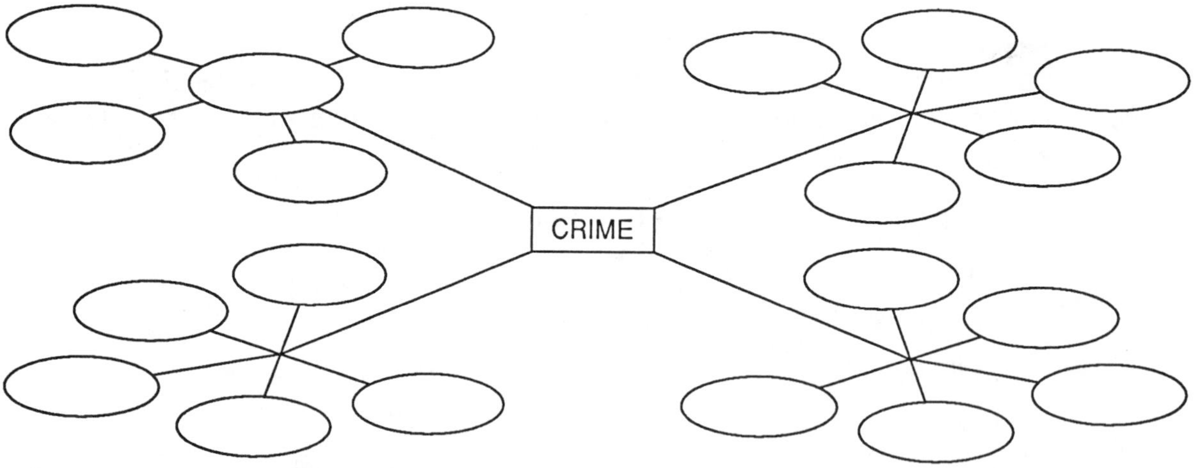

10 The words below are related to the law. Write them in the correct column below.

obey the law	break the law	enforce the law
against the law	legal	illegal

Good	Bad
1. ____________	1. ____________
2. ____________	2. ____________
3. ____________	3. ____________

11 **A.** The words in this unit frequently appear in newspaper articles. Bring to class an article about crime from an English-language newspaper. How many words from this unit are in the article?

B. Work in groups and write a newspaper article using as many words from this unit as possible. The group that correctly uses the most words will be the winner.

WORD STUDY

FOCUS ON CHOOSING THE CORRECT MEANING: One word in English can have many meanings. Therefore, it is important when using a dictionary to scan all the definitions for a word before deciding which definition is the one you want.

12 Below are three dictionary entries for words used in the reading on page 153. Find these words in the reading and read the sentences in which they occur. Then scan the dictionary entries. Underline the definitions which match the meanings of the words as they are used in the reading.

charge *v* **1** [I;T] to ask in payment: *The hotel charged me $30 for a room for the night.* **2** [T] to record (something) to someone's debt: *I'll charge the ticket and pay later.* **3** [I;T *at, towards,* etc.] to rush in or as if in an attack: *Suddenly the wild animal charged at us.* **4** [T *with*] to make a spoken or written statement blaming a person for breaking the law or for doing something morally wrong: *He was charged with stealing the jewels.* **5** [I;T] to (cause to) take in the correct amount of electricity: *The battery needs to be charged.*

sen·tence *n* **1** a group of words that forms a statement, command, exclamation, or question, usually contains a subject and a verb, and (in writing) begins with a capital letter and ends with one of the marks: . ! ? **2** a punishment for a criminal found guilty in court: *The sentence was ten years in prison.*

tri·al *n* **1** [C;U] (an act of) hearing and judging a person or case in a court: *The trial lasted six weeks.* **2** [C;U] (an act of) testing to find quality, value, usefulness, etc.: *She took the car* **on trial.** (= for a short time, to test it) **3** [C] a cause of worry or trouble: *That child is a trial to his parents.*

FOCUS ON THE PRONUNCIATION OF DERIVED FORMS: Many words have the same noun and verb forms, for example *to convict* and *a convict*. Some of these pairs have the same pronunciation, for example *to **mur**der* /'mɜrdər/ and *a **mur**der* /'mɜrdər/. However, other pairs have different pronunciations. Frequently, the stress in the verb is on the second syllable, as in *to con**vict*** /kən'vɪkt/. The stress in the noun is on the first syllable, as in *a **con**vict* /'kɑn vɪkt/. Note how the change in stress causes a change in the vowel sounds.

13 **A.** Use your dictionary to check the pronunciation of these nouns and verbs. Put a check (✔) next to the nouns and verbs which have the same pronunciation.

1. an arrest — to arrest ______
2. a convict — to convict ______
3. a permit — to permit ______
4. a sentence — to sentence ______
5. a suspect — to suspect ______

B. Underline the syllable of the word in *italics* which receives the stress.

Example: Two *<u>con</u>victs* escaped from prison last night.
The woman was *con<u>vict</u>ed* of robbery.

1. In most states of the United States, you must have a *permit* to own a gun.
2. In other countries, only the police are *permitted* to have a handgun.
3. The police *suspect* that the opera singer's husband murdered her.
4. The police are looking for one *suspect* in the murder of the opera singer.

REVIEW 4

1 Some words have a positive meaning. For example, if you are comfortable, you have enough money to live well. Therefore, *comfortable* has a positive meaning. Other words have a negative meaning. For example, people who are convicted of a crime often go to jail. Therefore, *convict* has a negative meaning. Finally, some words have a neutral meaning. They have neither a positive nor a negative meaning.

Do the following words have a positive, a negative, or a neutral meaning? Check (✓) the appropriate column. When you have finished, compare answers with another student. You may disagree, so be sure to give the reasons for your answers.

	Positive	**Negative**	**Neutral**
1. charge	______	______	______
2. fee	______	______	______
3. invest	______	______	______
4. reasonable	______	______	______
5. refund	______	______	______
6. wealthy	______	______	______
7. withdraw	______	______	______
8. claim responsibility	______	______	______
9. devote	______	______	______
10. iron	______	______	______
11. routine	______	______	______
12. take out the trash	______	______	______
13. task	______	______	______
14. break the law	______	______	______
15. enforce the law	______	______	______
16. innocent	______	______	______
17. sentence	______	______	______
18. stand trial	______	______	______

2 How well do you know the derived forms of the words you studied in Units 10, 11, and 12? Read each dialogue. Complete the sentences with the correct form of the words in *italics*.

1. *accuse*

   A: Who made the ____________________?

   B: I don't know. The police haven't said.

2. *crime*

   A: Do you think that a person who steals from the rich and gives to the poor is a ____________________?

   B: Well, stealing is a crime, isn't it?

3. *convict*

   A: The police are looking for an escaped ____________________.

   B: I hope they find him soon.

4. *responsibility*

   A: Who's ____________________ for this?

   B: Not me. I had nothing to do with it.

5. *charge*

   A: What's the ____________________, sir?

   B: We're arresting you for robbery.

6. *trial*

   A: They are going to ____________________ 85-year-old Emily Jenkins for killing her husband.

   B: But he was very sick and wanted her to kill him. How can that be murder?

7. *punishment*

   A: Should we ____________________ the children for breaking the car window?

   B: Absolutely. Let's make them pay for the new window.

8. *afford*

   A: Haven't you found a place to live yet?

   B: No. It's really difficult to find ____________________ housing.

9. *innocent*

   A: It's more difficult to prove your ____________________ after you've been arrested.

   B: You're right. That's why it's important to have a good lawyer.

3 Look at the words in the box below. If a friend asked you what they mean, how would you teach them to your friend? Would you show a picture? Would you give an example? Would you demonstrate the meaning? Would you give a definition?

Write each word from the box in the appropriate column. When you have finished, compare lists with other students.

Example: A picture: *sweep*—
An example: *against the law*—stealing, not paying taxes
A demonstration: *iron*—stand up and pretend you are ironing
A definition: *imprison*—put someone in prison

broke	well-off	support
can't afford	chore	accuse
moderately	mop	commit
receipt	set the table	offense

Show a Picture	Give an Example	Demonstrate the Meaning	Give a Definition

4 **A.** The word *charge* appeared in Units 10, 11, and 12. In each unit it had a different meaning. Read the following sentences. In which unit was *charge* used with this meaning? Write *Unit 10, Unit 11,* or *Unit 12* in the blanks. (Note: You will have to write one of the unit numbers twice.)

1. Did women agree to take charge of cooking and cleaning? __________
2. I charge $125 an hour. __________
3. People charged with a crime had to pay for their own imprisonment.

   ____
4. Is there a charge to have the sweater gift wrapped? __________

B. There are two dictionary entries for *charge.* One entry is for the verb, and the other entry is for the noun. Scan the entries. Write the number of the correct entry and the correct definition in the blanks following each sentence below.

charge[1] /tʃardʒ/ *v* **charged, charging 1** [I;T] to ask in payment: *How much do you charge for your eggs?|The hotel charged me $30 for a room for the night.* –see COST (USAGE) **2** [T] to record (something) to someone's debt: *Don't forget to charge the money to my account.|I'll charge the ticket and pay later.* **3** [I;T *at, towards,* etc.] to rush in or as if in an attack: *Suddenly the wild animal charged at us.|The children charged out of school.* **4** [T *with*] to bring a CHARGE[2] (4) against; ACCUSE: *He was charged with stealing the jewels.|He was charged last night.* **5** [T+*to-v*] *fml* to command; give as a responsibility: *She charged me to look after her son.* **6** [I;T] to (cause to) take in the correct amount of electricity: *Does your car* BATTERY (1) *charge easily?*

charge[2] *n* **1** [C] the price asked or paid for goods or a service: *This store has a charge for delivery service.|What are the charges in this hotel?* **2** [U *of*] care; control; responsibility: *I'm* **in charge of** *this department.|She* **took charge of** *the family business when her father died.* **3** [C] *fml* a person or thing for which one is responsible: *I became my uncle's charge after my father's death.* **4** [C] a spoken or written statement blaming a person for breaking the law or for doing something morally wrong: *He was arrested* **on a charge of** *murder.|The police* **brought a charge** *of murder* **against** *him.|He* **faces a charge** *of murder.* **5** [C] a rushing forceful attack **6** [C] the amount of explosive to be fired at one time **7** [C;U] (a quantity of) electricity put into a BATTERY (1) or other electrical apparatus

	Entry	**Definition**
1. He was charged with murder.	__________	____________________
2. I think you charged me too much.	__________	____________________
3. The teacher asked me to take charge of the class before she left the room.	__________	____________________
4. There's no charge. We do it for free.	__________	____________________
5. He's in serious trouble. He's in jail on a charge of robbery.	__________	____________________

C. Look at the remaining definitions of *charge* on page 164. Underline the other meanings of the word that you know.

D. Use the grammar information given with the dictionary entries for *charge* and decide which of the following sentences are correct. Circle the correct answers.

1. a. Who's in charge here?
b. Who's in a charge here?

2. a. He's spent three weeks in jail on charge of kidnapping.
b. He's spent three weeks in jail on a charge of kidnapping.

3. a. I didn't know there was charge. How much is it?
b. I didn't know there was a charge. How much is it?

4. a. Who's in charge of doing the laundry this week?
b. Who's in charge for doing the laundry this week?

5. a. They charged with shoplifting.
b. They charged her with shoplifting.

6. a. She was charged for bank robbery.
b. She was charged with bank robbery.

5 Rewrite each sentence using the word in parentheses. Do not change the meaning.

1. What you've done is illegal. *(law)*
What you've done is against the law.
____

2. Miriam was raised in Puerto Rico. *(grow up)*
____

3. Mr. Sawyer is responsible for hiring new workers. *(charge)*
____

4. I don't think you should pay $50 for that shirt. *(worth)*
____

5. We don't have enough money to buy a new television. *(afford)*
____

6. Do I have to pay for this? *(charge)*
____

7. She has spent all of her life taking care of the poor. *(devote)*
____

8. You must do what the law says. *(obey)*

____

9. The jury decided Ernest Wall was innocent. *(find)*

____

10. They said he stole their car. *(accuse)*

____

6 Play the game on the following page in groups of four. Each player uses a different box of words. Player A uses the words in box A, Player B uses the words in box B, Player C uses the words in box C, and Player D uses the words in box D. The number next to each word in the boxes is the point value of that word. Player A begins by writing down one of the words from his or her box next to *money* in the middle of the board. Then Player A must explain the connection between *money* and the word he or she has written down.

Example: *inherit/money* — I know a woman who inherited a lot of money from a relative she had never even met.

If the other players think that Player A's explanation is logical, he or she gets the points for using that word. (For example, if Player A uses *inherit* with *money,* he or she gets three points.) Then Player B writes down one of the words from his or her box next to *money* or next to the word Player A wrote down and explains the connection. (For example, if Player B uses *deposit* with *inherit,* he or she gets five points, but if Player B uses *deposit* with *money,* he or she gets only two points because *money* has no point value.) Player C can write down his or her word next to any one of the words already on the board and explain the connection. The game is over when players cannot use any of the remaining words in their boxes. The player with the most points is the winner.

A	B	C	D
comfortable 1	deposit 2	earn 1	high price 1
inherit 3	make a living 2	working class 2	possession 3
value 3	waste 1	dust 1	worth 3
accept responsibility 3	care 1	illegal 2	domestic 3
do the laundry 1	well-to-do 3	full responsibility 3	grow up 1
household 2	partial responsibility 3	raise 3	share 2
be found guilty 2	be on trial 3	charge 4	convict 4
fine 4	take charge of 4	imprison 3	obey the law 2

				MONEY				

AMERICAN LANGUAGE COMMUNICATION CENTER
PENNSYLVANIA HOTEL
7th Ave. Between W.32st. & W.33st.
NEW YORK, NY 10001
TEL: 1-800-ENGLISH

PAYMENT #: 1/AA0132946

DATE: 02/26/97 TIME: 13:42:00

STUDENT'S NAME: VIVAS,ROSA VIRGINIA
CARD: A46491 REP.: MARCELA

TYPE	$ PAID
F.PYMT	560.00

MY NAME IS: VIVAS ROSA VIRGINIA
TODAY I PAID: $ 560.00

STUDENT'S SIGNATURE Rosa Vivas

OPERATOR: CECILIA ESTEVEZ

SIGNATURE________________

...tory again. On a piece of paper write down what

...d many words in the last three units. They are

Unit 11	Unit 12
accept responsibility	accuse
be in charge of	be against the law
bring up	be on trial
care	break the law
chore	charge
claim responsibility	commit
devote	convict
do the laundry	enforce the law
domestic	find someone guilty
dust	fine
full responsibility	illegal
grow up	imprison
household	innocent

Unit 10	Unit 11	Unit 12
moderately	iron	obey the law
possession	mop	offense
reasonable	partial responsibility	sentence
receipt	raise	stand trial
refund	routine	
value	set the table	
waste	share	
wealthy	support	
well-off	sweep	
well-to-do	take charge of	
withdraw	take out the trash	
worth	task	
	vacuum	

B. It is difficult to remember and to use all of these words equally well. For example, some of the words you may be using already. Some of the words you may know the meaning of but are not comfortable using. Other words you may not remember at all. To help you check how well you know these words, write each of them in one of the following columns.

I Can Use These Words Correctly	I Know the Meaning of These Words, But I Can't Use Them Yet	I Think I Know the Meaning of These Words, But I'm Not Sure	I Don't Know These Words

C. You have probably found when learning new vocabulary that you do not always remember the same words after you have studied them. Words you think you know one week you can't remember at all the next week. Or this week you find yourself using words that last week you thought you didn't know. Look back at your columns of words on pages 43, 85, and 126. Do you want to move any of the words to a different column? If you do, why don't you make a new list? (From time to time, check your lists to see if there are any words you want to move to a different column.)

ANSWER KEY

Unit 1

3. a. 4 b. 1 c. 5 d. 3 e. 2
6. 2. c 3. a 4. b 5. c 6. a 7. b 8. a 9. b 10. a
7. 1. got annoyed 2. argument 3. yell 4. furious 5. grab 6. shatter 7. scream 8. slam
8. *Feelings of Anger:* annoyed, furious
Words Sometimes Connected with Anger: be in a bad mood, yell, grab, shatter, scream, slam
Words Always Connected with Anger: to have an argument, to lose your temper
10A. 1. a 2. a 3. a 4. b
B. 1. b 2. a 3. b 4. a
14B. 1. [C] 2. [T] 3. for 4. on 5. [U] 6. [I] 7. at
15. angered, angering; annoyed, annoying; grabbed, grabbing; screamed, screaming; shattered, shattering; shouted, shouting; slammed, slamming; yelled, yelling

Unit 2

2. c
3. 2. n 3. n 4. v 5. adj 6. adj 7. adj 8. v 9. v 10. adj
4A. 2. d 3. c 4. e 5. a 6. g 7. f 8. i 9. j 10. h
7A. 2. gratitude 3. gratefully 4. irritation 5. irritate 6. morality 7. morally 8. obligation 9. relieved 10. relief 11. sympathy 12. sympathize
B. 1. obligation 2. sympathy 3. gratitude (*or* relief) 4. relief (*or* gratitude) 5. morally 6. duty
8. 1. b 2. a 3. b 4. b
10B. 3. ay, say 4. o, horse; a, car 5. a, banana 6. a, car 7. i, bit 8. ea, beat
11. 1. Second 2. First 3. First 4. First 5. First 6. Second
12B. 1. No 2. Yes 3. No 4. No 5. Yes 6. Yes
13A. *Do:* someone a favor; a good job; something wrong; one's duty
Make: an excuse; a decision; a mistake; a promise; money; friends

Unit 3

1. 1. gas pedal 2. brake 5. turn signal 8. steering wheel 12. headlights 15. windshield wipers
2. 1. a 2. b 3. b 4. b 5. b 6. a 7. b 8. a 9. b 10. a
3. 1. No 2. Yes 3. No 4. Yes 5. Yes 6. No 7. Yes
4. (Possible Answers) 1. I was driving along the road. There was a truck behind me and we were coming to a sharp curve. At that moment, the truck moved into the other lane to pass me even though he couldn't see there was another car coming in the other direction. 2. I was going forty miles per hour. 3. The truck was probably going about sixty. 4. No, I slowed down so he could pass. 5. I steered to the right. 6. The other car also steered to the right, but the truck maintained its speed and ran into the car.
6B. 2. d 3. b 4. f 5. g 6. c 7. a
8. 3. clutch 4. horn 6. rearview mirror 7. sideview mirror 9. gear shift 10. speedometer 11. ignition 13. hood 14. windshield 16. trunk 17. bumper 18. tire 19. license plate
9A. 2. parking light 3. parking ticket 4. parking lot 5. parking meter 6. traffic jam 7. traffic sign 8. traffic light 9. traffic ticket 10. speed limit 11. headlight 12. stop sign 13. stop-light 14. car crash 15. gas station
B. 1. car crash 2. parking ticket (*or* traffic ticket) 3. stop sign 4. traffic

jam 5. parking space 6. gas station 7. parking meter 8. traffic light (*or* stoplight) 9. speed limit

11B. 1. She got into the taxi and left. 2. Robert usually picks up his wife at the subway station. Robert usually picks his wife up at the subway station. 3. The taxi driver dropped off Dr. Norton at her office. The taxi driver dropped Dr. Norton off at her office. 4. How could you forget to turn off the engine? How could you forget to turn the engine off? 5. The bus ran over the dog. The bus ran the dog over. 6. We turned off the highway at the first exit. 7. I can't believe you ran into a police car!

12. 3. turned it off 4. got into it 5. picked me up 6. dropped me off

Review 1

2. 1. argue 2. dutiful 3. gratitude 4. relief 5. morally 6. sympathize 7. sympathy 8. obligation

4. 1. up 2. up, down 3. up 4. off 5. off 6. through 7. into 8. over 9. down 10. up

5. 2. She loses her temper easily. 3. You went through the stop sign without stopping. 4. It wasn't my fault. 5. I'm in a great mood today. 6. He has a guilty conscience about what he did to his friend. 7. I can't stand driving in the center of town. 8. I'm not in the mood to do it.

7. See tapescript.

Unit 4

2. 1. F 2. F 3. T

3. 2, 5

4. 1. b 2. a 3. b 4. a 5. a 6. a 7. b 8. a 9. b 10. a

6B. 1. a slight (*or* mild) pain in my back 2. a terrible (*or* bad, severe, *or* an awful) headache 3. a major (*or* serious) illness 4. an awful (*or* a bad, terrible) cold 5. a slight headache 6. a minor illness 7. a slight cold 8. a sharp (*or* bad, terrible, severe, *or* an awful) pain 9. slightly ill

7A. (Possible Answers)
Usually Not Serious: the flu, indigestion, diarrhea, constipation, a rash, a cold
Serious: diabetes, heart attack, a stroke, AIDS, cancer, high blood pressure

8. a. 5 b. 4 c. 1 d. 6 e. 2 f. 3

9B. (Possible Answers) 2. *avoid:* 1, 3, 4, 5, 6, 7, 9 3. *catch:* 1, 9 4. *cure* (5) 6, 7 5. *get:* 1, 2, 4, 5, 6, 7, 8, 9 5. *get over:* 1, 2, 5, 9 6. *have:* all 7. *relieve:* 2, 5 8. *treat:* all

10A. 2. avoidable 3. exposure 4. infection 5. infectious (*or* infected) 6. spread 7. treatment 8. treatable 9. cure 10. curable 11. painful

B.

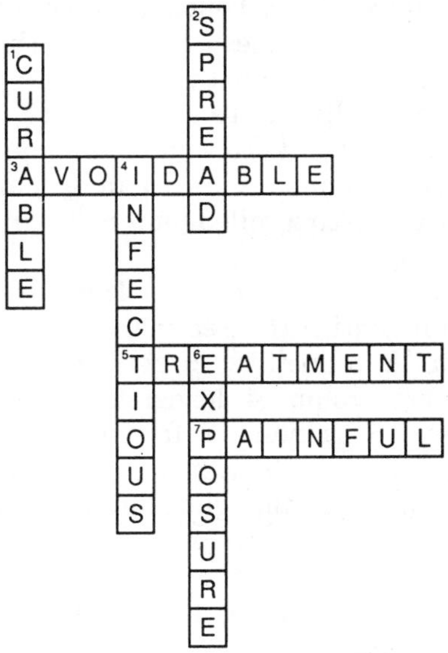

12B. 1. + *v-ing* 2. caught 3. [T] 4. to 5. with 6. spread

13A. *Sounds like bed:* dead, headache, spread, breath, health
Sounds like meat: earache, disease, ease, breathe, treat, heal

B. *Sounds like I'm:* diabetes, diarrhea, prescribe, virus, diet
Sounds like sit: disease, medical, sick, dizzy, examine, prescription

Unit 5

2. All the statements are true.

3. 1. No 2. Yes 3. Yes 4. Yes 5. No

5A. (Possible Answers) 1. change what happens; have an effect on 2. dependable; doing what one says one will do 3. a person you are with; a person you do things with 4. having strong feelings; related to feelings 5. the condition of something; how good or bad something is 6. the way a person or an animal acts 7. go to for help 8. a feeling of unhappiness because you are alone 9. help; advantage; good point 10. act or behave towards a person

B. (Possible Answers) 1. cause/change 2. says/will do something/she'll do it 3. someone/do things with/because/alone 4. love/hate/strong feelings 5. never happy/condition/sick 6. way you acted 7. problem/go/ask for help/need 8. suffer/however/lonely/unhappy 9. good/one/feel safer/however/disadvantages 10. talk to them/things/people do with

7B. 1. To an ally 2. To a co-worker 3. To a classmate 4. To some company 5. To a teammate 6. To an acquaintance 7. To a colleague 8. To an accomplice

8. 2. benefit 3. beneficial 4. lonely 5. influential 6. treatment 7. emotion 8. reliability 9. rely on

9A. 3. partnership 4. leadership 5. kindness 6. sadness 7. friendliness 8. friendship 9. selfishness 10. relationship 11. thoughtfulness 12. laziness

11A. 1. b 2. d 3. c 4. e 5. a

13. 1. 4 2. 1 3. 2 4. 4 5. 1 6. 3

14A. *bene: good*

B. 1. benefactor 2. benediction

Unit 6

2. Words which generally refer only to marriage: wedding, spouse, divorce

3. According to what the speaker said in the interview, he would agree with statements 2, 3, and 4

5A. 2. j 3. h 4. a 5. b 6. g 7. f 8. i 9. d 10. e

7B. 2. e 3. d 4. f 5. c 6. a

8A. 1. a boyfriend to his girlfriend 2. Shelley and Vince 3a. go with 3b. go out with 3c. go with 4a. Andrea and Charlie 4b. Date someone 5a. Husband and wife 5b. No

B. 1. "I love you" and "I'm in love with you" both show the person has very strong feeling for the other person, but "I'm in love with you" also means there is a strong sexual attraction and desire. 2. *Date someone* means "spend time frequently with someone, usually of the opposite sex." *Have a date* refers to one specific event. 3. *Go out with* and *go with* can both mean "have a relationship with someone of the opposite sex for a period of time." 4. *Go out with* can also mean "spend time with someone, of the same or opposite sex, on one particular occasion." *Go with* does not have this meaning. 5. *Separate* can refer only to a married couple not yet divorced. *Separate, break up,* and *split up* can refer to all couples with a long relationship. Married couples that have *broken up* and *split up* are usually divorced.

9. (Possible Answers) a. 11 b. 5 c. 2 d. 9 e. 4 f. 6 g. 3 h. 8 i. 1 j. 14 k. 12 l. 13 m. 7 n. 10

12B. 1. 3 2. 1 3. 1 4. 2

13. 1. proposal 2. proposition 3. proposal 4. respectable 5. respectful

14A. relation; relations; relationship; relative (*also possible:* relativity)

B. 1. relatives (*or* relations) 2. relationship 3. relations

Review 2

2. 1. avoidable 2. curable 3. exposure 4. infection 5. spread 6. treatment 7. companionship 8. beneficial 9. reliability 10. rely 11. influential 12. behaved

4. 1. to 2. with 3. up 4. up 5. up 6. over 7. for 8. along 9. out

5. 1. b 2. a 3. b 4. a 5. a 6. b

7. See tapescript.

Unit 7

3. c

4. 1, 3, 4

5. 1. a 2. b 3. b 4. b 5. a 6. b 7. b 8. b 9. a 10. a

7B. 1. nationalists 2. a feminist 3. a sexist 4. racists 5. terrorists

6. nationalists 7. environmentalists 8. a communist 9. capitalists

9A. environmentalists

B. 2. ban 3. marchers 4. protest 5. demonstration

10. 1. vote 3. opposition 4. opponent 5. protest 6. protester 7. campaign 8. demonstrator 9. demonstrate 10. elect 11. govern 12. march 13. march 14. politics 15. political 16. eligibility 17. qualification 18. qualify

12. 2. 4,2 3. 2,3 4. 3,2 5. 5,2 6. 3,1

13A. disagree, qualified, eligible, nonelected

B. disagree, disapprove, dishonest; incomplete, ineligible, inexperienced; nonelected, nonmember, nonprofit; uneducated, unqualified, unsuccessful

C.

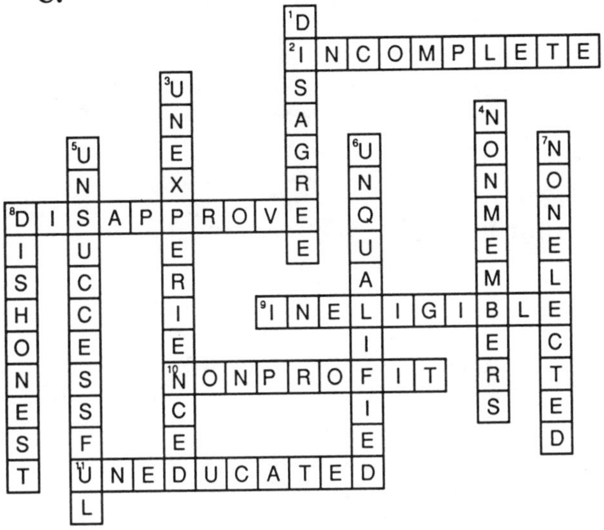

Unit 8

2. (Possible Answers) 4. U 5. U 6. U 7. BOTH 8. U 9. U 10. N 11. BOTH

3. b

4. 3, 4

6A. 1. not pass an examination or course; be unsuccessful in 2. unable to understand; mixed up 3. very smart 4. have a clear meaning 5. sign a piece of paper to show one is going to take part 6. stop taking 7. related to teaching or studying, especially at a university 8. be necessary 9. consisting of many parts which can make something difficult 10. easy to understand

B. (Possible Answers) 1. difficult/don't understand/70/pass 2. don't understand/explain 3. smart/but/so intelligent 4. meaning/understand/explain 5. take the course/paper/wait . . . won't be able 6. hated/not . . . going to do well/after two weeks/not taking it anymore 7. prepared . . . college/but/typing and driving classes 8. but you don't have to 9. difficult/several parts/take me time to find the answer 10. only one part/easy

7. 1a. didn't do well 1b. failed 2a. intelligent 2b. brilliant 3a. register 3b sign up 4. complicated, difficult 5. Simple, easy

9A. *A:* class, course *B:* class *C:* educational *D:* scholarship *E:* academic *F:* homework

B. 1. assign and mark homework 2. academic record 3. cut class 4. a partial scholarship 5. an academic scholarship

10. dumb slow average smart bright brilliant

11B. *USA:* 3, 4, 5, 7, 8, 9, 10, 12, 13, 14

13A. *Get:* a bad grade, a high school diploma, a scholarship, a university degree, 523 on the TOEFL, a certificate
Take: a course, a test, a break

14. 1. bored 2. interesting 3. tiring 4. tired 5. confused 6. shocked 7. confusing 8. boring 9. interested 10. shocking

Unit 9

3A. 1. American 2. Japanese 3. Japanese 4. American 5. Japanese 6. American

4B. 1. employer; manager 2. staff 3. fire; lay off 4. firm 5. position 6. hire 7. economic 8. industry

C. (Possible Answers) 1. got the job/start next Monday 2. secretarial/job 3. company/also 4. workers had complained I was unfriendly/didn't think I was the right person for the job 5. car/clothing/30 percent of the people in the area work in these factories 6. pay their workers/give jobs 7. happy with your work/However/bad news/company . . . having problems/people/afraid you are one of them 8. companies closed down/businesses in trouble/difficult for people to find work 9. solved my problem quickly/her workers/make sure it didn't happen again 10. everyone who works here

6A. *At the beginning:* hire, get a job
In the middle: I've gotten a promotion., go on strike, get a raise
At the end: You're fired., lay off, retire, lose my job, quit

7B. (Possible Answers) 1. Occupation is a more formal word than job. 2. A profession requires special training and a high level of education, but work doesn't always require this. 3. An occupation is work, but a career is work that you do all your life. 4. The staff consists of a number of employees at a workplace. 5. Workers work with their hands, but employees may or may not work with their hands. Employees is a more general word. 6. People receive a salary every two weeks or every month, but people receive wages every week. 7. A salary is money you receive for work. An income is also money you receive on a regular basis; it can be money received for work, but it doesn't have to be. 8. Fire is a more informal word than lay off and, when you are laid off, it is often because business at the place where you are working is not good.

8A. 2. economic 3. economical 4. economist 5. economy 6. economize

B. 1. unemployed 2. unemployment 3. employees 4. employed 5. employment 6. employer

10B. 1. a 2. — 3. — 4. a 5. — 6. — 7. a

11A. Cross out: *go, look.*
2. reschedule 4. rewrite 5. redo 6. retell 7. reread 8. rebuild 10. retype

B. 1. rehire 2. rewrite (*also possible:* redo, reread, retype) 3. redo 4. retell (*also possible:* rewrite, reread, retype) 5. rebuild 6. reread (*also possible:* rewrite, retype) 7. reschedule 8. retype (*also possible:* rewrite, redo, reread)

C. X: 1, 3, 4, 5

Review 3

2. 1. economical 2. economize 3. employed 4. employment 5. demonstrators 6. opposition 7. opponent 8. qualifications 9. vote 10. protesters

4. 1. unemployed 2. disagree 3. inexperienced 4. ineligible 5. retype 6. redo 7. dishonest 8. nonmembers

5. 2. They don't have the right to get married without their parents' permission. 3. The teacher assigned so much homework. 4. I've been laid off. 5. You're eligible to apply for the scholarship. 6. Nothing makes sense. 7. I failed the test. 8. I attend every class. 9. The government has banned cars from the downtown area.

7. See tapescript.

Unit 10

2. 1, 3, 4, 5

4A. 1. charge 2. fee 3. can't afford 4. well-off (*or* wealthy) 5. possessions 6. value 7. wealthy (*or* well-off) 8. Middle-class 9. make a living 10. broke

B. 2. b 3. c 4. a 5. c 6. b 7. b 8. a 9. a 10. c

6A. *Money Coming into Your Pocket:* inherit, earn, withdraw, save, make, steal, borrow
Money Going out of Your Pocket: spend, waste, lend, invest, deposit

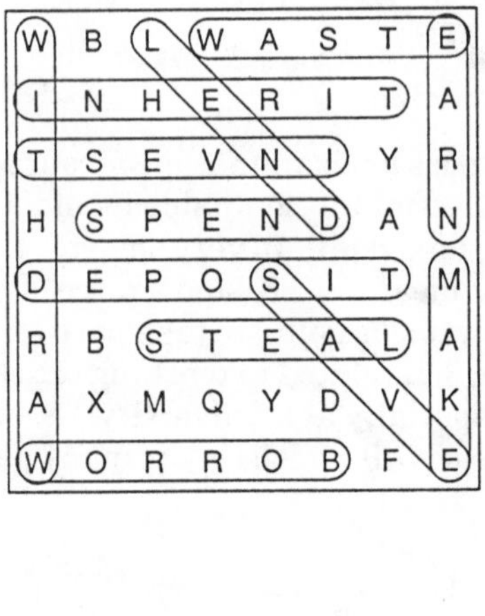

7A. 1. e, a 2. c, d, f, b

B. expensive; It's worth $50; there's no charge; the receipt; a full refund; reasonable; The price is reasonable; a charge

8. 1. (Possible Answer)

cheap / inexpensive — reasonable — moderately expensive — expensive / high

2. (Possible Answer)

poor — comfortable — well-off / well-to-do — wealthy

3. (Possible Answer)

lower class — lower middle-class / working class — middle class — upper middle-class — upper class

10. (Possible Answers) 2. A friend of mine who is broke wants to borrow some money. 6. My brother who is well-off is going to lend me some money.

11A. 1, 3, 4, 5

Unit 11

3. 1. 1737: Men and women; 1911: Mostly men 2. 1737: Nobody; 1911: Mostly women 3. 1737: Men and women; 1911: Mostly men 4. 1737: Nobody; 1911: Mostly women 5. 1737: Nobody; 1911: Mostly women

4B. 1. support 2. routine 3. tasks 4. domestic 5. raise 6. shared 7. care 8. take charge 9. devoted 10. responsibilities

C. (Possible Answers) 1. the act of looking after a person or thing 2. taking a lot of care of someone or something 3. of the home or family 4. help to grow 5. having the duty of looking after someone or something and accepting blame if something goes wrong 6. the regular unchanging way of doing things 7. use or have with others 8. give money for (a person) to live on 9. control 10. (some) hard work

7A. 2. take charge of 3. be partly responsible for 4. accept full responsibility for 5. be in charge of 6. take partial responsibility for 7. claim responsibility for

B. 1. have, accept, take, claim 2. full, partial 3. partly 4. for

9A. 1. raise 2. grow up 3. bring up 4. grow up 5. *Grow up* cannot be passive

B. 1. task 2. chore 3. chore 4. No

C. (Possible Answers) 1. a husband and wife 2. a washing machine 3. food 4. a housekeeper or a maid 5. A husband has hit his wife or a wife has shot her husband.

D. 1. care for 2. b

10A. 1. mop the floor (wash the floor) 2. wash the clothes 3. buy food and other things for the house 4. wash the dishes 5. wash the windows 6. cook dinner

C. 1. *make the bed:* sheet, blanket, pillow 2. *do the dishes:* soap, water, dishwasher 3. *set the table:* dish, silverware 4. *sweep the floor:* dustpan, broom 5. *mop the floor:* mop, soap, water, bucket 6. *dust:* dustcloth 7. *vacuum:* vacuum cleaner 8. *iron:* iron, ironing board 9. *take out the trash:* trashcan 10. *do the laundry:* soap, water, washing machine 11. *clean the bathroom:* soap, water

12. 1. b 2. a 3. b 4. c

13A. 2. able; ability 3. domestic; domesticity 4. fatal; fatality 5. legal; legality 6. moral; morality 7. reliable; reliability 8. simple; simplicity 9. stable; stability 10. stupid; stupidity

B. In nouns ending in *-ity,* the stress is usually on the third syllable from the end.

C. 1. /e^y/; /ə/ 2. /t̬l/; /tæl/ 3. /ə/; /æ/ 4. /ə/ ; /æ/ 5. /e^y/; /ə/

Unit 12

1A. 1. d 2. b 3. e 4. f 5. h 6. g 7. a 8. c

2. 1. F 2. T 3. T

3. ✓: 3, 5 (These are implied.) DS: 1, 2, 4, 6

5A. 1. charged with (*or* accused of) 2. accused of (*or* charged with) 3. commit 4. trial 5. innocent 6. convicted of 7. sentence 8. fine 9. offense 10. imprisoned

B. 1. prison 2. pay money 3. wrong 4. crime 5. wrong 6. trial 7. serious 8a. done something wrong, committed a crime 8b. committed a crime

6A. A: find someone, be B: stand, be on C: a crime, suicide

7. a. 2 b. 1 c. 4 d. 6 e. 5 f. 3

8. 2. offender 3. punish 4. try 5. accusation 6. charge 7. conviction 8. convict 9. fine 10. imprisonment 11. sentence 12. innocence

10. (Possible Answers)
Good: obey the law, legal, enforce the law
Bad: against the law, break the law, illegal

12. *charge:* to make a spoken or written statement blaming a person for breaking the law or for doing something morally wrong
sentence: a punishment for a criminal found guilty in court
trial: (an act of) hearing and judging a person or case in a court

13A. 1, 4

B. 1. permit 2. permitted 3. suspect 4. suspect

Review 4

2. 1. accusation 2. criminal 3. convict 4. responsible 5. charge 6. try 7. punish 8. affordable 9. innocence

4A. 1. Unit 11 2. Unit 10 3. Unit 12 4. Unit 10

B. 1. 1; 4 2. 1; 1 3. 2; 2 4. 2; 1 5. 2; 4

D. 1. a 2. b 3. b 4. a 5. b 6. b

5. 2. Miriam grew up in Puerto Rico. 3. Mr. Sawyer is in charge of hiring new workers. 4. I don't think that shirt is worth $50. 5. We can't afford a new television. 6. Is there a charge for this? 7. She has devoted her life to taking care of the poor. 8. You must obey the law. 9. The jury found Ernest Wall innocent. 10. They accused him of stealing their car.

7. See tapescript.

TAPESCRIPT FOR REVIEW UNITS

Review 1

My life is a full and happy one, and I'm grateful for all I've been given. However, I could never call my life perfect when I see so many poor, hungry, and homeless people around me. They put up with more difficulties in their lives than I will ever know, and none of it is their fault. How can my conscience not bother me? Isn't it my moral duty to help them? I feel that I'm obligated to do something and blame myself every day for doing nothing. But what one thing can I do to relieve their pain? Can anyone tell me? Can you?

Review 2

I fell for her the moment I saw her. It was on the beach near a colleague's home where I met her. I can't say what attracted me to her, but we got along right from the start. We went out every night for two very romantic weeks. Two weeks after we started dating, I proposed to her. Three weeks later we were married. We've been in love for fifteen years now, and she treats me like a king. We have a stable marriage, we respect each other, and we turn to one another whenever we have a problem. Who could ask for anything more? She's been a great influence in my life. That day on the beach was the luckiest day of my life.

Review 3

My college requires that business majors like me take a political science course in order to graduate. When I signed up for one last spring, I had no idea I would be a candidate for President in the 2064 election. But then I didn't know I had registered for Professor Home's course. First, we had to decide what we thought would be the important political and economic issues in the future and then we formed political parties. For the rest of the course, we attended meetings with the other people in our party and worked on our campaign. It was hard work but a lot of fun. It was probably the best course I ever took.

Review 4

Many of today's middle-class parents are not raising their children the way they were brought up. Their mothers usually stayed at home with them and were in charge of the household tasks, and their fathers left home every morning to go out and make a living. However, because these days both parents are responsible for supporting the family, children spend a lot of time by themselves. When parents are at home, they're so busy with domestic chores that it's difficult for them to find the time they need to devote to their children. While yesterday's parents couldn't afford to waste money, today's parents can't afford to waste time.

INDEX

CREDITS

Page 2, adapted extract from pp. 82–84, *Eat This . . . It'll Make You Feel Better* by Dom DeLuise. New York: Pocket Books. © 1988 by Petmida, Incorporated. Pages 15–16, adapted from "What Are Your Values and Goals?" *Psychology Today*, May 1989. © 1989 by PT Partners. Page 28, adapted from "Are You A Good Driver?" by Joan Rattner Heilman. *Parade Magazine,* March 18, 1990. © 1990 by Parade Publications, Inc. Page 46, adapted from "The Cold Facts," *Healthwise,* editor Mary Alice Czerwonka, Minneapolis: Riverside Medical Center. Page 59, adapted from "Influence of Pets Reaches New High" by Lena Williams. *New York Times,* August 17, 1988. © 1988 by The New York Times Company. Page 70, adapted from "The Folly of Romantic Love" by Cynthia Lollar. *Special Report*, Aug./Oct. 1990. © 1990 by Special Report, Whittle Communications, 505 Market St., Knoxville, TN 37902. Page 88, adapted extract from pp. 683–684, "Support Democracy: End Elections" *People's Almanac #3* by David Wallechinsky and Irving Wallace. New York: William Morrow & Co. © 1981 by David Wallechinsky and Irving Wallace. Page 98, adapted extract from pp. 33–36, *The Good Times* by Russell Baker. New York: William Morrow & Co. © 1989 by Russell Baker. Page 109, adapted from "Do It My Way," *The Economist,* November 24, 1990. © 1990 by The Economist Newspaper, NA, Incorporated. Pages 114 and 164 excerpted from *Longman Dictionary of American English* reprinted with permission. Page 129, adapted extract from pp. 2–14, *Money Talks: How Americans Get It. Spend It. Use It and Abuse It* by Walter Wagner. Indianapolis/New York: The Bobbs-Merrill Co., Inc. ©1978 by Walter Wagner. Page 140, adapted from "Domestic Chores Weren't Always Women's Work" by Debbie Taylor. *New Internationalist,* March 1988. Page 153, adapted from "How Did Our Prisons Get That Way?" by Roger T. Pray. *American Heritage,* July/August 1987. © 1978 by Forbes, Inc.